"*Fit Matters* offers hope, inspiration, and practical tools for finding joy, meaning, and engagement at work."

— **Daniel Pink,** author of *Drive* and *To Sell Is Human*

"A must-read for anyone looking for their next amazing opportunity or who wants to tweak their current situation to make the fit just a bit better."

— **Pat Wadors,** SVP, Global Talent Organization, LinkedIn

"Carrick and Dunaway's book powerfully illustrates the importance of 'getting in where you fit in' if you want to flourish at work. While many people think they understand opportunity-fit, this book will reveal surprising categories of job-fit that must all be taken into account. Read this book if you want to find the career of your dreams, not the bane of your existence."

— **Tim Sanders,** *New York Times* bestselling author of *Love is The Killer App: How To Win Business and Influence Friends*

"We should all love our jobs – and what Carrick and Dunaway prove is that we all can. This isn't a soft option – it means everyone has to bring their A game to work every day. But when they do, work fulfills its great ambition: the fulfillment of human life."

— **Margaret Heffernan,** author of *Beyond Measure* and *A Bigger Prize*

"You can be happy, even joyous, in your job if it's the right fit. By showing you how to tap into your core professional and personal values, *Fit Matters* is your can't-miss guide to great career satisfaction!"

— **Marshall Goldsmith,** *New York Times* bestselling author of *Triggers*

"Imagine working for a company that has the culture and environment that allows you to bring your "Best Self" to work. STOP imagining, leverage the wisdom and tools in *Fit Matters,* and get closer to your best self. The book is also a great guide for managers and leaders who want to build world-class teams!"

— **Annie Young-Scrivner,** EVP, Starbucks and Board of Directors, Macy's Inc.

"Finding the right fit at work can be truly life changing – opening up a path to greater joy, impact, and success. Carrick and Dunaway have developed an excellent guide to identifying that right fit and making it happen, with practical tips to help each step of the way. If you want to make a change to increase your happiness and achieve your full potential, then *Fit Matters* is the book for you."
— **Jen Dulski,** CEO, Change.org

"Whether you are mid-career, retired and contemplating what's next, or just starting out, this guidebook is a great choice to help find a role that brings you true joy. Full of practical, pivotal, and pithy advice and actionable assessments to discover your path from purpose to fulfillment."

— **Denny Post,** CEO and President, Red Robin

"Finding a good match is just as important for the employee as it is for the employer. As an employee, when you find your fit you deliver the best results and create attractive growth and career opportunities. For organizations, finding the right employees is key to accomplishing the company's mission, vision, values, and giving you your best business performance. *Fit Matters* shows you how."

— **Xavier Lopez Ancona,** Founder and CEO, KidZania

"Fit matters. When the fit isn't there it impacts many factors, one of the most important is centered around inclusion. When you don't feel like a true member of the team due to fit you are often made to feel like an outsider. When one feels like an outsider it can impact our self-esteem, self-confidence, and, over time, can impact our performance impact. Before taking on a new job, do your homework. Don't take the job if there is a mis-alignment to what is important to you. *Fit Matters* offers inspiration and ideas for ensuring that you find positive work fit."

— **Michelle Clements,** Vice President, Human Resources, Seattle University

"Few decisions in life are more important than finding a great fit for your professional life. It should be no surprise that the most effective leaders I find are the ones who truly love what they do. Your team, your customers, and even your family will know when you find a great match and are passionate about your work. Why wait? This timely book offers wonderful advice on how to thrive at work. A must read!"

> — **Greg Welch,** Sr. Partner at the executive search firm Spencer Stuart

"Our happiness as humans is what drives our desire to achieve more which makes it crucial to find the right fit in any career. Cammie and Moe did a superb job in breaking this down into more than just a book, but a handbook you can keep with you to create a meaningful approach to loving what you do."

> — **Bryan Kramer,** TED Speaker, author of *Shareology* and *Human to Human: #H2H*

"I believe that fit is one of the most important and least understood aspects of work. It can make the difference between extraordinary success and satisfaction, or unexpected derailment and discontent. Today, when we expect employees to own their careers, recognizing what you personally need in order to thrive is essential. This book helps unlock some of the mystery and provides practical advice that will help people make better, more informed decisions about the opportunities they choose to pursue."

> — **Sekhar Ramaswamy,** Chief Talent Officer, Prudential Financial

"Being demoralized at work is one of the most life sapping experiences people can face – we spend inordinate amounts of time and mental energy doing our work and if the fit isn't right, our lives often don't work well overall. Understanding what a great fit looks like and how to find yourself in that place will undoubtedly energize, revitalize, and make you a happier and more empowered person. This book will be the guide for your journey."

> — **Shannon Stowell,** President and CEO of the Adventure Travel Trade Association

"It is unfortunate how many people are disengaged at work. We live in a time where you *can* work a company that aligns with your values and sense of purpose and your work is no longer a job but rather a calling. This is a profound difference, which authors Carrick and Dunaway understand completely. *Fit Matters* provides the road map for your great work fit!"

— **Scott Allan,** General Manager Hydroflask

"*Fit Matters* is a must-read for anyone trying to build out a values-based and culture-laden team, as well as those seeking out a job with personal and professional purpose and meaning."

— **Scott M. Davis,** Chief Growth Officer, Prophet Consulting

"I learned while leading the People Department at Southwest Airlines the power of working where your personality and values fit the company culture. When that happens, work feels more like life versus drudgery. Following the inspirational advice of Carrick and Dunaway will lead to a more purposeful life and a fulfilling career."

— **Libby Sartain,** author *HR from the Heart* and *Brand from the Inside*

"Moe Carrick and Cammie Dunaway are masterful in offering practical and inspiring guidance on what it takes to thrive at work in a role that fits. Their recipe of six essential elements is a time-tested resource you can turn to again and again."

— **Virginia Klamon,** Ph.D., Executive Leadership Coach and Business Owner

FIT
MATTERS

FIT
MATTERS

HOW TO LOVE YOUR JOB

MOE CARRICK
CAMMIE DUNAWAY

MAVEN HOUSE

Published by Maven House Press, 4 Snead Ct., Palmyra, VA 22963; 610.883.7988; www.mavenhousepress.com.

Special discounts on bulk quantities of Maven House Press books are available to corporations, professional associations, and other organizations. For details contact the publisher.

While this publication is designed to provide accurate and authoritative information in regard to the subject matter covered, it is sold with the understanding that the publisher is not engaged in rendering legal, accounting, or other professional service. If legal advice or other expert assistance is required, the services of a competent professional person should be sought. — From the Declaration of Principles jointly adopted by a Committee of the American Bar Association and a Committee of Publishers and Associations

Library of Congress Control Number: 2017900165

Hardcover ISBN: 978-1-938548-74-1
ePUB ISBN: 978-1-938548-75-8
ePDF ISBN: 978-1-938548-76-5
Kindle ISBN: 978-1-938548-77-2

Printed in the United States of America.

10 9 8 7 6 5 4 3 2 1

DEDICATION

To everyone suffering at work with misery and discontent,
we offer hope: there is a workplace for you.
Carry on, because your gifts and talents matter somewhere.

To the organizational leaders that strive to create workplaces fit for
human life – thank you. Your reward is people who come to work
everyday bringing their highest and best to your workplace,
which as you know, is so very worth it.

And for our children and their children:
may your work challenge you, touch your heart
and excite your mind on more days than not.

To see takes time. — Georgia O'Keefe

CONTENTS

Appendices

ACKNOWLEDGEMENTS

WE BOTH FEEL CHANGED by the process of writing this book. We entered it naïve to the world of publishing but activated about the possibility of helping more people thrive at work. The journey has been at times arduous and, simultaneously, wondrous. Our North Star has been our shared conviction that people can and should thrive at work, not suffer or simply count time. Human beings all over the world need to work for a whole host of reasons, including our basic human desire to contribute to something bigger than ourselves – to matter.

Right at the top of the list of people to thank are our families. They put up with countless weekend and evening hours of us tied to the computer and on the phone digging and learning when we could have been spending time with them. They have each encouraged us and humored us by listening to sections, talking through structure, and applauding our efforts even when we were struggling. Their unconditional support of us has mattered more than anything. Lendy, Jim, Ian, Davis, Cam, and Hannah – thank you. And our parents, Margaret Vaughn and Dan Luechauer, Pat and Richard Whisnant, we thank you for providing the faith and confidence in us individually since we were tiny girls that we could do it, whatever it was. Your love and belief in us has always made a difference.

Our journey has brought hundreds of stories into our lives of individuals struggling to find a job that makes their heart sing as well as those who get up every day excited about going to work. To the hundreds of people we interviewed and surveyed, we thank you so much for sharing your stories with us. It helped shape and affirm our thinking and our approach, and we recognize how deeply personal your experiences have been. Understanding your journeys has mattered greatly to our creation of this book.

Our reader team provided countless hours of document review and edits – thank you for your wisdom, candor, and feedback: Jason Zazzi, Deborah Holstein, Sarah Marsh, Jim Morris, Barbara McAfee,

ACKNOWLEDGEMENTS

Marietta Cozzi, Sekhar Ramaswanmy, Ron Fritz, Nick Besbee, Barbara Lish, Anita Bhasin, Joan Perry, Jacki Ross, Krista Calvo, Michelle Clemens, Virgina Klamon, Rebecca Perry, Kim Moon, and Darren Pleasance. And special thanks to Ian Carrick, Cameron Carrick, and Lori King for their special help with research and editing at crucial junctures in our process when we needed an extra lift and pair of hands. This work is better for what you brought.

From the beginning we were graced with the faith and optimism of our amazing agent, Kelli Christiansen. Thank you for believing in us and helping us stay buoyed in the face of rejection. You are so good at what you do, and we have benefited hugely from your wisdom. Our Publisher and Editor, Jim Pennypacker of Maven House Press, and his team provided countless patient words of wisdom throughout the process of bringing this book forward. Your grace and patience, combined with your absolute surety that we had something good to say to the world, has made this process truly joyful.

And finally, thank you to our clients and employers both past and present. It is through our work with you that we have seen, firsthand, what great work fit looks like and how it feels when it is nonexistent or not a priority. Each of you, alongside employers everywhere, are the ones who set the tone and the stage for bringing out the absolute best in each person who works for you or in creating disengaged people. This privilege is gargantuan, and we thank you for showing us the myriad opportunities and pitfalls inherent in the employer/employee relationship.

FOREWORD

A S HEAD OF HR FOR LINKEDIN, I care deeply about how we find and attract amazing talent for our company. Not just any talented person will thrive at LinkedIn – we seek people who are right for us, and whose motivation, needs, interests, and skills are suited for what we have to offer. As an employer, it benefits us to spend time and energy carefully assessing the nature of the right fit with each candidate. This is hard, because we, like most companies, often want to sell the role or the company, and yet experience shows us that the effort of assessing fit will ensure the best success for us and the potential employee. In addition, when we have candidates who clearly know themselves and are prepared to evaluate us as an employer that will bring out their best, it's much easier to place them in roles, teams, and environments where they will thrive.

Fit does matter! You deserve to love your job and bring your best authentic self to work every day. Companies benefit when each person who works there is highly engaged and aligned with the organization's purpose and culture. When the fit is right, there's real joy for the employee and a tangible business upside in both individual and team performance.

Despite our best efforts, we sometimes get it wrong. Employers in general must get it wrong a lot because a recent Gallup study revealed that only a third of workers say that they're engaged in their current job (Rigoni and Nelson 2016). The risks are high that any employer, including LinkedIn, will hire the wrong person in the wrong job or in the wrong company at the wrong time. When this happens, it's expensive in time, energy, and mindset for everyone. There are so many things that come into play to make the right fit – timing, experience, personality, financial needs, passion, background, lifestyle requirements, social style, and motivation, to name a few. I believe that even though getting it right is complex and not always a straight shot, we all deserve to be happy and successful where we work, and companies deserve to have engaged and motivated employees bringing their best every day.

I appreciate the work that Carrick and Dunaway have done in this book to untangle the algorithm for finding fit. *Fit Matters: How to Love Your Job* is pragmatic in its approach and helps all of us to evaluate ourselves and our needs for work in order to up the odds that we can secure a workplace that suits us well. The authors share the relationship between six essential elements of fit, explore the dynamic and interrelated nature of those elements, and help you to measure your fit as a critical step in enhancing your current job or landing the right job for you. Their practical and honest frameworks opened up my thinking and gave me new ways to evaluate real fit. Some of it was intuitive, but the authors' research and stories added a much richer level of awareness for me as a leader. I found insights and questions that will serve me well on our path at LinkedIn to assessing candidate fit, as well as help me to think about my own fit and that of my employees at every job stage.

I believe this book will help employers and employees, as well as job seekers, to increase their work satisfaction, engagement, and happiness. Thank you to Carrick and Dunaway for their wisdom and insight. The stories in the book enlivened the approach for me, and I think everyone will find themselves somewhere in the pages, which I hope will provide hope, reassurance, and ideas. This is a must-read for anyone looking for their next amazing opportunity or who wants to tweak their current situation to make the fit just a bit better.

Work is such an important part of our lives, and at LinkedIn, we seek to connect the world's professionals to make them more productive and successful. Ensuring that the job you take is a great fit for you is key to becoming effective, successful, and content. I highly recommend this book for your fit journey at work!

Pat Wadors
Senior Vice President
Global Talent Organization
LinkedIn

PREFACE

THE FACT THAT YOU PICKED UP THIS BOOK means that something about your current work fit may be calling for your attention. Perhaps you're in a job that looks great on the outside, but day in and day out you're struggling. Or maybe you're just now entering the workforce and want to find the perfect place to add value. Possibly you dream of a different work experience that meets more of your personal needs. Maybe you're a coach, an HR (human resources) professional, manager, or recruiter who helps people define and secure their right job. Or maybe you just have a nagging feeling that there could be a more fulfilling option out there that's better than your current work-life situation.

Most of us spend a lot of time at our jobs. We spend more hours in any given week earning a living than just about anything else: sleeping, eating, playing, creating, exercising, parenting, dreaming, or gardening.

When our jobs fulfill us, we thrive. But when our jobs fail us, we languish.

That's why this book matters, and why we wrote it. We know from our personal and professional experience that the match between employee and employer matters in tangible and intangible ways that are far more comprehensive, important, and material than can ever be measured. What would happen for all of us, and for the world, if more people actually loved their jobs?

We met in a professional situation that had at its center a workplace misfit. Cammie, in a significant job change, joined Nintendo of America in what looked from the outside to be the perfect situation: Executive Vice President of Sales and Marketing. In her capacity as a coach to the executive team of the company, Moe began to work with Cammie to help her integrate with the team and lead her huge division. At first the job seemed a match made in heaven. Cammie entered as an experienced leader with big ideas for innovation and expanding the company's reach to new consumers. The work was stimulating and the team welcoming and supportive. But over time cracks started to appear.

Coming from Silicon Valley, Cammie was used to running an agile organization where team members could experiment without fear. She thrives in environments that encourage open and rigorous debate around new ideas and the empowerment of team members.

What she began to observe at Nintendo was a very cautious approach to building relationships. There was a system of rigorous checks and balances that reduced the chance of a bad decision, but seemed painfully slow compared to the nimble culture to which she was accustomed. Subtle differences in how decisions were made and performance was evaluated began to discomfit Cammie. She saw things one way, and sometimes it seemed that she was alone among the executives in her viewpoint. Her confidence in her ability to be heard and to make an impact waned. At first, she told herself that she was the problem, and that if she just worked harder to fit in and adjust, it would work out. She didn't want to feel like a quitter. Plus, she had good friends at work and the company made amazing products. But the harder she tried to shift her style, the harder the work became and the less passion she had for the job. Despite the dream that this job would be a career capstone for her, she finally acknowledged (with the help of Moe, her coach) that staying was exacting too high a price and that it was time to move on. Leaving her job in just three years wasn't the outcome she expected, but Cammie knew as soon as she made the decision that it was right. She went on to find a better work fit and the result was higher satisfaction, more daily joy, and, ultimately, better results for Cammie and her new organization.

In her thirty-plus years consulting to organizations and individuals, Moe has encountered case after case of job misery – people who find that their daily world of work has become, in essence, a fortress of struggle, dissatisfaction, low esteem, unhappiness, and drudgery. They often revealed stories of disillusionment and pain, frequently with an opening sentence such as, "I feel like such a failure that it's not working out for me here." The stories revealed countless negative impacts, ranging from poor physical health to shattered families, from sleepless nights to overwhelming worry and fear.

From the employer's point of view, countless company leaders we've known over the years have talked about the costs of misfit in a key role. These leaders faced mountainous challenges in realigning people, finding new talent, and recruiting the perfect-fit employee – only to have them leave too soon.

When a job isn't right for you, you suffer, your family suffers, your community suffers, your company suffers – even the world at large suffers. Stress rises and performance falls, resulting in lower-quality work and performance, which affects the bottom line in a not-so-virtuous cycle of dissatisfaction and diminishment (ADAA 2006).

We believe that there's a better way, which is why we wrote this book.

The process for finding a great work fit is neither easy nor simple. Most of us spend precious little time understanding and considering fit when we take a job, which often costs us time, energy, and job satisfaction down the line. We propose that work fit is dynamic and temporal. That it consists of six essential elements, where fit expands and contracts for each of the elements based on what stage of life you're in. Understanding the relationship between these elements of fit, and developing resilience in assessing and measuring your fit in each of them, is key to landing the right job for you.

Our combined research, life experiences, and conversations with employees, bosses, and company owners have convinced us that the world will be better when work fit is a high priority for both employee and employer. And perhaps more importantly to you, a great work fit will enliven your days, improve your outlook, and remind you of your unique and valuable contributions.

In this book, we offer what we believe is a key ingredient for work that's essential for you today and tomorrow: hope. The hope that, for most of the days you spend working, you'll feel good. The hope that meaning and value and contribution will be yours more often than not, resulting in greater alignment, satisfaction, and joy.

To get there you need to know yourself deeply, and you need to know how to assess the unique qualities that organizations possess. Looking beyond the marketing buzz of best places to work, we lay out a pragmatic and personalized method for you to discover what will work for you, with which company, at which time in your life. The world has big problems to solve, and organizations will play a big role in solving them by having the right people in the right jobs. So let's dig in and find the right fit for you.

Note: We've included Ask Yourself boxes to help you get the most out of this book. We suggest you keep a notebook or an open page on your tablet or computer to reflect on these questions and track your progress.

ASK YOURSELF

- Why did I pick up this book?
- How do I feel about my current work situation?
- How clear am I on understanding my own strengths, needs, and weaknesses?
- What is it that I want to learn more about or discover regarding work fit?

PART I

WHAT FIT MEANS

CHAPTER 1

Understanding Fit

People who love their work bring an intensity and enthusiasm that is impossible to match through sheer diligence.

— Gretchen Rubin, The Happiness Project

JOHN REACHED OVER and pushed the snooze button once again. It's been getting harder and harder to get out of bed in the morning. He has a big presentation today and a meeting with his boss, and he's dreading both. The job seemed perfect at first, but in two years it's deteriorated to the point where John wonders if he should update his resume and start looking for a new job. His team is functioning poorly and their results are poor. Tension is high between John and his boss because their values are no longer in sync. He doesn't want to share these problems with his wife because he knows she'll worry. There aren't a lot of jobs in his field in their town; they just moved his wife's mother to a nursing home nearby, and John feels increasingly trapped. Slowly he drags himself out of bed, dreading another day.

Just about everyone can relate to John, occasionally feeling dissatisfied, frustrated, and even disillusioned with the company they work for. John really hoped to fit at his company, and to happily retire from there one day. Instead, he's checked out, looking for a job elsewhere, and clearly not bringing his A game to his current work. John's stress level is high, and it's starting to show in his relationships at home. What had started out as a match made in heaven – the perfect job – has exploded into a burned-out executive and a job search, expensive for both John and his company.

It's a familiar tale. In more than thirty years of consulting to organizations and leading teams, we've heard story after story of genuine anguish and frustration from people who suffer in jobs and companies that aren't right for them.

Everyone deserves to love their job, and it starts with having a great fit between you and the organization where you work. But, as we said earlier, finding a great fit is neither simple nor easy.

You're Not Alone

If you find yourself struggling with fit at work or longing for more meaning in your job, you're not alone. According to The Conference Board Job Satisfaction Survey (Kan et al. 2016), less than half of U.S. workers are satisfied with their jobs. And a recent Gallup study revealed that only a third of workers say that they're engaged in their current job (Rigoni and Nelson 2016). Unfortunately, instead of pursuing the belief that everyone deserves to be happy and fulfilled in a job for which they're a great fit, many people just give up on the pursuit of job satisfaction, buying into the false belief that work is just a necessary evil, something you have to do to pay the bills.

Why do so many of us simply accept unhappiness and dissatisfaction as natural elements of work? How do people end up in companies that rob them of satisfaction and even joy? Why do they stay? What are the costs for people and organizations of poor fit alignment? What measures can be taken to increase the odds of landing at a company that's the right fit for you? What should you do if you're suffering at work because of misfit?

We started asking a lot of questions in preparing to write this book. And we found a lot of answers. We found survey data, research, real-world stories, tools, and exercises that not only shed light on why so much unhappiness exists but also on what people – people like you – can do about it. Through our years of experience in consulting to and leading organizations, combined with our research of more than 500 people and over 50 interviews, we've culled potent stories of fit and misfit, as well as trends that shaped our thinking. You'll hear the voices of the people we talked with throughout the book. We also offer ideas and inspiration that will help you take heart and keep searching for a job that's the right one for you at your particular stage of life. There's a company out there that's a great match for you, and when you find it both you and your organization will benefit.

What Is Work Fit?

We define *work fit* as the degree to which a job with a particular company fits you – how well the job's requirements and the company's values and culture mesh with your expectations, values, personality, and skills. Broadly speaking, it's the match between an employee and the company for which they work. A great fit at work is akin to that perfect pair of jeans that goes on easy and makes you feel good in your own skin. We know it when we find it, but the search is often long and frustrating, and many employees in the United States and around the world haven't found it, settling instead into jobs they keep for financial motivation – but little else.

It's critical to emphasize that great work fit isn't about looking alike or being part of the same social group, class, race, or gender, often called "fitting in." It's about having a common set of values, desires, and expectations that allow you to bring your best self to work.

When work fit is poor, a job feels like this, said Stacy: "The role was lacking in any opportunities for growth or even a lateral move. There was zero flexibility and employees were micro-managed – phone calls were listened to and timed, and even bathroom breaks were timed. It felt like a people factory, not a team environment. It felt like I was punching a time clock and my contributions and ideas didn't matter." And Andrea said, "Every day felt like 'damned if you do, damned if you don't' because it seemed like nothing I did was ever enough to please my management. In one case, this happened even when I did as much as I could with as few resources as possible."

Figure 1-1 is a word cloud showing what people said about poor work fit, or misfit, in a survey we conducted.

When work fit is great, a job feels like this, said Billye: "I have felt pleasure in my job since the beginning. The joy and pleasure of the work

Poor Work Fit Word Cloud

Figure 1-1. This word cloud depicts what respondents said about poor work fit, or misfit, in a survey conducted by the authors.

made the difficulties easier. I share beauty with the world; I'm a salesperson and I love, admire, and appreciate what I sell. I feel that I'm helping to enable people who create beauty to make money and sell a product that gives joy and long-term pleasure."

Figure 1-2 is a word cloud that shows how our survey respondents felt about great work fit.

ASK YOURSELF . . .

- Have I had a work experience that was a great fit? What was it like?

- How did I know?

- Which words from either word cloud resonate with me and why?

- What have been the implications for my happiness, health, and well-being at work and at home when I've been in a great work fit or misfit situation?

Great Work Fit Word Cloud

Figure 1-2. This word cloud depicts what respondents said about great work fit in a survey conducted by the authors.

Everyone Needs – and Deserves – Great Work Fit

People are not machines. As humans, we're hardwired to garner a personal sense of value and purpose through our work. Standard thinking about human needs places meaningful work, which is connected to self-esteem and self-actualization, near the top of the ladder, behind physiological and safety needs. Current researchers and thinkers have elevated connection to others, engagement, and contribution as even more basic to our humanity, closer to our most basic needs for food and shelter.

Researcher, author, and TED notable Brené Brown (2010) emphasizes the importance of wholeheartedness (the capacity to engage in our lives with authenticity). She says that connection and belonging – both of which are needs we bring to the places we work – are as important as other basic human needs. Similarly, Patrick Lencioni (2002), blockbuster author on teams and organizations, suggests that, more than anything else at work, people crave being seen and valued and feeling like they contribute to work that matters (in any role at any level).

Healthy workplaces and great fit between employee and employer are critical to activating great performance and powerful human connections. We believe that everyone can enjoy great work fit, but finding the right match is challenging since people and workplaces are unique.

Professionals in the United States and worldwide spend a great deal of time at work – more than they do sleeping, eating, playing, engaging in household activities, or with family and friends (U.S. Department of Labor 2014). For many of us today, a large number of our needs must be met in the workplaces we join, so happiness in life largely correlates to happiness at work. When you feel good at work, you have energy and the capacity for creativity and partnership. This in turn creates a virtuous cycle in which the better you feel, the more you contribute to work results. People are drawn to partner with you, and together you get things done well.

Changing jobs is exhausting, but the toll taken from continuing in an environment that's a misfit is incredibly high. Poor work fit erodes employee health and well-being, which leads to stress-related illness, stress on families, and stress among coworkers. We know that stress manifests itself in chronic long-term illnesses such as heart disease, diabetes, anxiety and depression, alcohol and drug abuse, and cancer. It also results in fractured family and community systems. These trends affect the health of employees, their quality of life, their relationships at home, and their efficacy in the communities in which they live.

A Better Way - The Virtuous Work Cycle

When you enjoy and feel successful at something – a hobby, a sport, a relationship – you look forward to it and want to devote time and energy to doing it well. And it's certainly the case with work. When you love the work you're doing, when it truly uses your skills and experiences in a positive way, it creates a virtuous cycle (see Figure 1-3). Because you enjoy your job, you don't mind working hard, and you're able to tackle challenges with confidence and enthusiasm. Your peers and bosses can see that you're going the extra mile to solve issues and generate ideas, and in turn they respond positively to your efforts. Simply put, the more you like your work the better work you do, the more positive feedback you receive, and the greater your enjoyment becomes.

The evidence, as well as our own experience, confirms that feeling good about work leads to better performance and greater success. Research by Jessica Pryce-Jones (2010) reveals that people who are happy at work:

- Get promoted more
- Earn more
- Get more support
- Generate better and more creative ideas
- Achieve goals faster
- Interact better with colleagues and bosses
- Receive superior reviews
- Learn more
- Achieve greater success

It makes sense – when you're happy and at ease you tend to be more productive. You're more open to learning new things and less frustrated by obstacles and challenges. This confidence means that you make fewer mistakes, and that you're more likely to learn from them. You can view problems as opportunities for growth rather than reinforcement of all the things that are wrong. When you're in a virtuous work cycle, relationships with coworkers and superiors go more smoothly. We're naturally attracted to people who enjoy what they're doing, and we're more likely to give them support or to seek out their input and involvement.

This happiness and sense of purpose spills out into our personal lives. Indeed, the connection between feelings about our work and satisfaction with our overall lives is supported by hundreds of articles and academic dissertations going back to the mid-1930s. One of the most far-reaching studies occurred in the 1970s, when Angus Campbell at the Institute for Social Research at the University of Michigan undertook a massive research project to understand how Americans defined the quality of their life experiences (marriage, parenting, health, etc.) and the impact of those experiences on the quality of their lives overall. Campbell found that satisfaction with work was one of the strongest predictors of overall well-being, accounting for almost a fifth of the variance among those

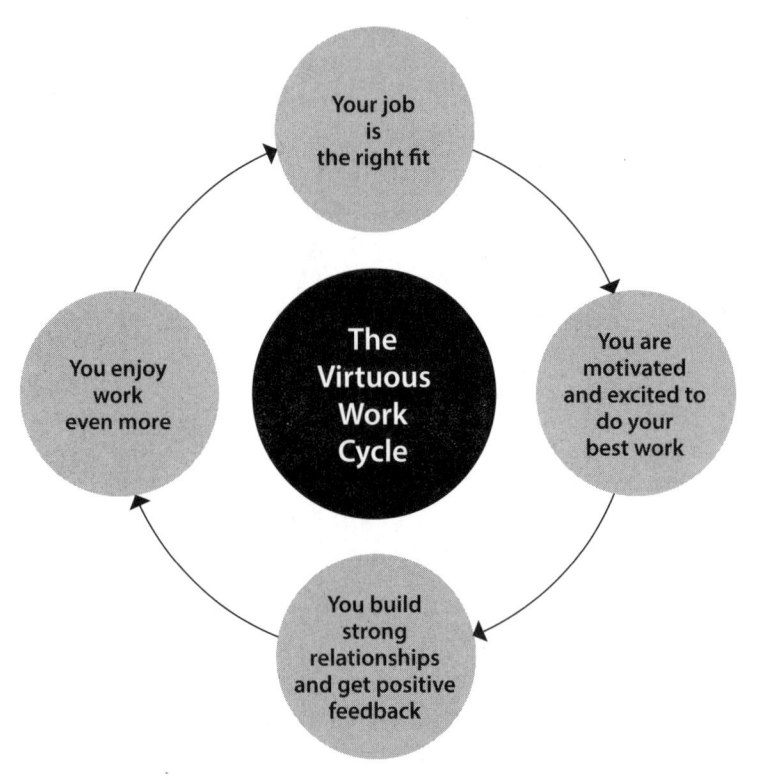

Figure 1-3. The virtuous work cycle is the result of loving your work.

who reported a high satisfaction with life and those who did not. Satisfaction with work was more important than satisfaction with finances and friendships, and equally important as satisfaction with family life (Campbell, Converse, and Rodgers 1976).

Organizations Need Great Work Fit

The costs of poor work fit are staggering. When an employee leaves after only a short employment stint, that vacancy leaves a wake of destruction. Many studies have shown that the total cost of losing an employee can range from tens of thousands of dollars to twice that person's annual salary (Bersin 2013). The cost of an employee leaving is astonishing.

But when employees stay in poor work fit situations the cost is even greater. It's expensive enough to replace an employee who leaves, but imagine what it costs when an underperforming employee doesn't leave but simply lingers on for years. By some estimates the loss of productivity due to employee disengagement costs between $450 billion and $550 billion per year in the United States alone (Gallup 2013).

Companies large and small simply do better when their employees are thriving. They make more money, accomplish their missions, produce more, engage happier customers, create less waste, make better innovations, and develop more productive vendor and partner alliances. For the foreseeable future, the human capital of organizations – the employees – will be the main factor in determining which companies will endure and which will churn and burn. Thus, it's good for business to ensure a good match between the employees and the culture of the organization. Period.

There Is a Path to the Right Fit

Take heart: great work fit is possible. There's a great fit for every job seeker and job provider; we know it ourselves and we've seen it happen for other people and other organizations.

Throughout these pages we'll share practical advice, reflective exercises, and real-world stories designed to help you advance your understanding of great work fit and how you can achieve it. We'll talk about the importance of getting to know yourself – and how you can go about doing just that. We'll explain the six essential elements of work fit, and we'll discuss how your prioritization of these elements changes over the course of your career, and how to weight them for yourself. And we'll look at how everyone can – and must – handle work misfit.

The Six Elements of Work Fit

We've identified six essential elements of work fit (see Figure 1-4). While it's unlikely that all of these elements are great at any point in time, we need at least some of them to be working well in order to feel that we fit well in our organization.

1. **Meaning Fit** – Meaning fit is great when you feel that what you do matters.

The Six Elements of Work Fit

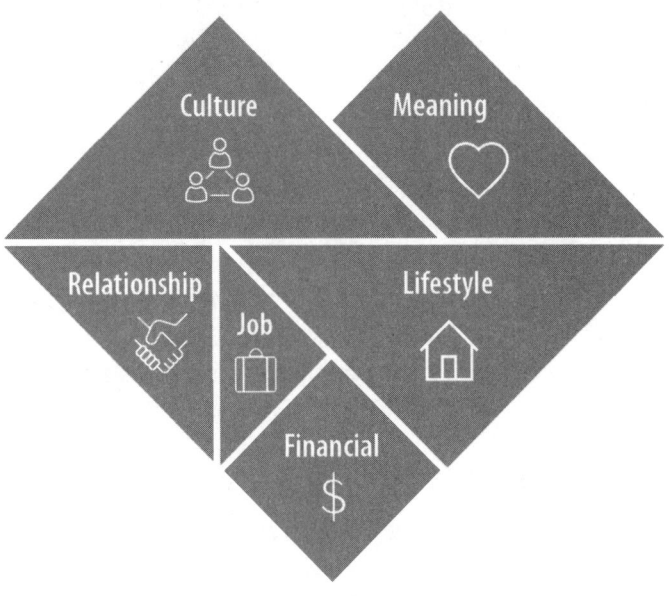

Figure 1-4. At least some of these elements of work fit need to be working well in order to feel that you fit well in your organization.

2. **Job Fit** – Job fit is great when the responsibilities of your job align with your talents and provide opportunities for growth.

3. **Culture Fit** – Culture fit is great when your values and beliefs are compatible with the practices of your employer.

4. **Relationship Fit** – Relationship fit is great when you like and respect the people you work with and receive appropriate support and trust to do your job.

5. **Lifestyle Fit** – Lifestyle fit is great when your life outside of work is supported by your employer's policies and practices.

6. **Financial Fit** – Financial fit is great when you feel that you're paid fairly and when what your employer offers (salary, bonus, benefits, perks, and allowances) meets your needs.

It takes effort to find the path to great fit – and to stay on it. For many of you it begins with asking the question, "How well do I fit in my current situation?" Or, "Am I thriving here?" Chapter 2 will assist you in recognizing whether you're a misfit today and start you on the path to great work fit.

It's time for a new way to work that's compatible with human health, well-being, and satisfaction, and is also good for business and productivity. Suffering in a job should *not* be an essential part of anyone's career path. Accordingly, we have created The Fit Manifesto (see Figure 1-5) as a guide and inspiration for individuals and organizations committed to ensuring great fit between people and their organizations.

The Fit Manifesto

1. It's possible to feel engaged, happy, and valued at work.

2. People are healthier in mind, heart, and soul when they feel satisfied in their jobs.

3. Individuals who find the right work fit do better outside of work and help create resilient families and strong communities.

4. Work fit varies based on time of life; needs change with circumstances.

5. Organizations do better in all ways (profit, performance, quality, mission) when employees are right for the work and the culture. Companies succeed when the people in them succeed.

6. There is a place for everyone to thrive at work. What works for one person might not work for another. The fit equation is highly personal.

7. A focus on work fit benefits people, organizations, communities, and the world.

8. Fit matters! The global economy demands that people everywhere feel connected and relevant so that they bring their best work to work.

Figure 1-5. The Fit Manifesto is a guide and inspiration for individuals and organizations committed to ensuring great fit between people and their organizations.

CHAPTER 2

Recognizing Misfit

When I let go of what I am, I become what I might be.
— Lao Tzu

FOR SOME OF US, there's a sudden, lightning-bolt moment when we realize that where we work is not aligned with who we are. For others, it takes longer to discover that it's not the right workplace. In either case, a moment comes when we realize that we just don't fit at our workplace anymore.

The dictionary describes a misfit as a person whose behavior or attitude sets them apart from others in an uncomfortably conspicuous way. In our experience, although being misfit at work may not always be conspicuous, it's always uncomfortable.

Tammy has experienced misfit firsthand. "During the interview process, I expressed my need and desire for flexibility since it was something I had at my current job. I also expressed my desired job role and how I felt I could contribute the most. I took the job, and within two weeks I knew it wasn't a fit. The culture was one of coworkers 'keeping score' – what time did someone come in/leave, how long did they take for lunch (remember that flexibility thing?). Didn't matter if work was getting done. The role was completely different from what was explained to me. I wasn't doing what I thought I'd be doing, and the work was boring, not challenging, and any opportunities I expressed to help the company in its efforts were shot down.

"I felt that my boss was dishonest with me in describing how the company operated. I now had a sour taste in my mouth because I left a job I loved for this one. I quit after four months – a great decision. During the six months that it took to find a new job I did some consulting work to help me get by. It was worth the wait. My current job is one of the best jobs I've ever had."

Tammy realized quickly that her new job was obviously a misfit. Sometimes, though, discomfort stemming from misfit comes with a more gradual realization that things just aren't working. Over time you may feel less enthusiastic about work, your performance reviews aren't as strong, your mind drifts during meetings, and you find yourself being short with colleagues. Perhaps you entered a new stage of life, such as becoming a parent, which caused a shift in your values. Or perhaps you'd mastered the basics of your job and craved new challenges.

Sometimes it's not you but the organization changing in ways that alter the work fit. It might happen when a boss leaves and is replaced by someone you see as incompetent or difficult to get along with. The company might be acquired by an organization with a vastly different culture, which happened to Jason: "I knew when we got bought out things would change. At first it seemed the acquiring company would preserve our culture and way of doing things, but as shared services began to occur and efficiencies became critical, the life got sucked out of our small company. I knew it was not going to be the right place for me for long."

Sometimes fit can be dramatically affected by a downturn in the business cycle. Perhaps a new senior leadership team makes major changes that affect the way employees interact and get work done. The circumstances can vary, but the outcome leaves you feeling like a foreigner in a place you used to enjoy.

This was the case for Pam. When she was in her early twenties she took a temporary job at a high-tech company, thinking that she would be there for a year and then return to grad school. She ended up staying for sixteen years and thriving for the first fourteen.

"What made me fall in love with the company was that I could speak up and voice my opinion and that if I had good ideas, management was all ears," Pam says. "My initial role was an entry-level position focused on tracking global inventory – basically I had a spreadsheet and a telephone. I immediately became interested in why certain policies existed and how we could do things better, and I started making suggestions. Pretty soon I found myself in meetings with vice presidents. I felt like my opinions mattered, and the supportive environment gave me the confidence to tackle bigger and bigger challenges. The company culture was focused on the customer and on getting things done. That really jelled with who I am and how I like to work."

Pam never left the company for grad school. For fourteen years she found herself getting promoted almost every year to positions of ever-expanding responsibility. Then things began to change. A more challenging business climate led to the internal environment becoming more political. Sharp elbows were thrown as execs jockeyed for position and power. A senior leader whom Pam admired was passed over for a major job and left the company. The remaining senior leaders were highly political and the culture of speaking up and championing new ideas disappeared. "Gradually more and more of the people I enjoyed working with left. It got so that I couldn't stand going into the office. I just couldn't muster the energy to give a damn about my work. And on top of that, I felt guilty about my feelings and a little disloyal to the company I had loved for so many years."

Pam realized that she needed to make a move so that she could continue to thrive and do her best work. Her job search lasted six months and led to a position with a young, fast-growing company where she again experienced the joy of knowing that her opinion mattered.

"The energy at my new company is palpable and contagious. People are smart, getting things done, and having fun. I feel like myself again."

How Bad Is It?

Let's be crystal clear: We all have bad days – even bad weeks – when we don't feel satisfied in our jobs. Every job in every company brings with it hard times, days when getting out of bed is a laborious chore, or times when team dynamics make it such that we dread seeing our colleagues in the halls or at the lunch table. Every supervisor can be the poster child for a bad boss on any given day, and every organization goes through life-cycles of progress and accomplishment as well as darkness and struggle.

One bad day or even a bad week doesn't necessarily mean that you and your job are suddenly incompatible. When you're misfit at work, discomfort spreads over months on end, and going to work seems like an insurmountable chore day after day. There's a difference between a bad spell and a serious case of your company no longer being the place for you. Our friend Katt describes it like this: "Leaving a company is never an easy decision, but when you wake up morning after morning hating your job, it's time for a change."

The signs of misfit can vary, but here are how several friends, clients, and survey respondents describe their symptoms:

1. **You dread going to work.**
   When you find that getting up is a chore and that you're living for the weekend, things aren't working. The root problem may stem from any number of factors, but the need for change is clearly being signaled.

2. **You're getting sick more often.**
   Our bodies frequently tell us we have a problem even before our minds acknowledge it. When people suffer from deep misfit, they often struggle with stress-related physical symptoms such as headaches, colds, heart palpitations, and general body aches and pains.

3. **You have trouble sleeping.**
   Insomnia has many causes, but if your inability to get a good night's sleep kicked in right when you started managing a more intense or difficult work situation, it's likely related. Stress-induced insomnia occurs when anxiety takes its toll on you so intensely that it robs you of your ability to sleep.

4. **You feel bored and underutilized.**
   If you find yourself watching the clock or spending more time on social media or other online channels during work hours, chances are you need more challenges or opportunities to contribute more of your skills.

5. **You don't like your boss and try to avoid them.**
   A poor relationship with your boss is one of the most common causes of misfit. This also probably means that you're getting

little in the way of the positive coaching or feedback that we all need to thrive.

6. **You can't think of anyone at work you enjoy spending time with.**
Work colleagues don't need to be best friends in order for you to be successful, but if you feel like you don't like anyone in your organization, chances are you need to move on.

7. **You're consistently getting poor performance reviews.**
When you're in the right job, you're able to do your best work. This doesn't mean that you won't make mistakes and face occasional failures, but it does mean that you should feel successful and supported.

8. **You don't feel valued.**
Feeling like your work matters is one of your most basic needs.

9. **You find yourself complaining a lot.**
If you catch yourself constantly complaining about work to your family, or even to another colleague, something needs to be addressed.

ASK YOURSELF . . .

- Which of the nine signs of misfit ring true for me, if any?
- How would I rate their intensity (1=low, 9=high)?
- What might be the implications for my happiness, health, and well-being at work and home?
- How might misfit be impacting my performance at work?
- Have I felt misfit before? How does this feel the same or different?

So What Now?

Once you acknowledge that you may be a misfit at work, the next step is to diagnose the source of the misalignment. While unhappiness can make it seem like everything about your job sucks, the reality is usually more complex and nuanced. Job content and corporate culture might be okay, but a new boss might be making you miserable. You may be unhappy with growth opportunities, but glad that your job allows the flexibility to work from home. By examining the six elements of work fit in Part II of this book, you'll be able to determine what specific elements of work fit aren't working for you and therefore what needs to change.

Moving forward in achieving great work fit also means getting a clear understanding of your needs and desires and having a process for understanding the trade-offs between the elements. Part III goes into detail about why fit matters. Part IV provides useful tools and exercises for self-reflection and decision making. And, finally, Part V provides tips to help you make the best of the situation that you're in when changing jobs isn't possible (at least not at the moment), or while you explore your options for moving to a different organization.

Everyone can and should find a job where they'll thrive rather than survive. Despite the fear and tension that admitting to misfit can bring and that recognizing that the journey to reach a better work fit might be a long one, we believe that the effort is worth it. Consider the words of Greg: "Deciding that this job was not in my long-term best interests was painful, stressful, and depressing. But looking back from the other side, it was wonderfully invigorating, spiritually fulfilling, and full of warm satisfaction."

Now is the time for you to start looking at the specific elements that create great work fit so that you can love your job!

PART II

THE SIX ELEMENTS OF FIT

CHAPTER 3

Meaning Fit

The key question to keep asking is, are you spending your time on the right things? Because time is all you have.

— Randy Pausch

MEANING MATTERS. The need to feel connected to a genuine and important purpose is fundamental to our overall human existence and is a critical element of truly loving your work. Doing what you love and following your passion works for some of us, some of the time. But for most of us, most of the time, the issue of meaning is more fundamental and reflects deeper issues than simple passion. Meaning fit, which we describe as knowing deep inside that what we do matters, is not only a crucial element to work fit, but also to overall human existence. Victor Frankl (1959), in his best-selling book, *Man's Search for Meaning,* concludes that meaning is at the very core of humanity's will to survive.

In the post-industrial age of service, professional, and information economies, meaning is increasingly becoming a primary element of the choices we make in our vocation. And many researchers conclude that, for young people (Millennials and the yet to be characterized Generation Z), the element of meaning in our work has risen to the top.

It makes sense to us. Belongingness and contributing to something that matters are basic human needs. A 2015 *Fast Company* story stated that "more than 50 percent of Millennials say they would take a pay cut to find work that matches their values, while 90 percent want to use their skills for good." We all seek ways to matter.

Nevertheless, many of us have yet to feel that potent and rewarding connection to purpose. According to the Centers for Disease Control and Prevention, four out of ten Americans have not yet discovered a satisfying sense of their purpose. Nearly a quarter of all Americans report feeling neutral or don't have a sense of what makes their lives meaningful. We believe that work itself can provide limitless opportunities to find meaning and purpose, and our research shows that the search for meaning in work is a significant driver for many people today. There is copious evidence that having a purpose and meaning increases our well-being. As Emila Esfahani Smith (2013) said in her article in *The Atlantic,* "Research has shown that having purpose and meaning in life increases overall well-being and life satisfaction, improves mental and physical health, enhances resiliency, enhances self-esteem, and decreases the chances of depression."

In our interviews, people's faces lit up when they talked about their jobs where they felt great fit for meaning. Often, once they got talking, we found ourselves basking in the delight of their joy, energy, and enthusiasm for doing work that mattered to them. As Hillary said, "It feels amazing to hear about the future of the company and know that I'll be a part of that future. I've found a place where I want to belong and I'm so thankful that I do."

In every job held by any human being, a connection to work that's seen by others and makes a difference is important. No matter how entry-level the work, we simply do better when we feel as if the effort we're making makes a difference to someone. It can be as simple as a supervisor who notices the extra effort we put in, or a CEO who gives us accountability and room to innovate.

Moe tells a story of discovering a higher purpose in a summer job as a hospital janitor. She learned just how important her somewhat dull and redundant work was when a patient died of an illness she contracted while in the hospital for a routine appendectomy. When Moe's boss explained to her how Mrs. Johnson had died, he reinforced that this was why it mattered so much that cleaning materials were applied in the correct order – bacteria and germs were complex and easy to miss when the

Aspects of Meaning that Affect Work Fit

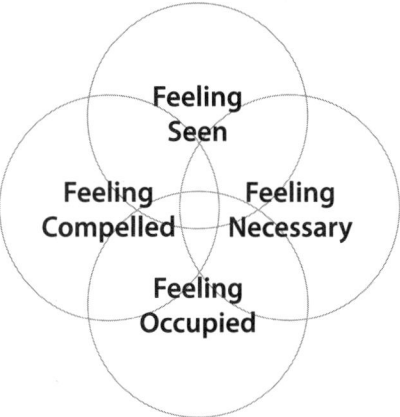

Figure 3-1. There are four interconnected aspects of meaning that affect work fit.

application was careless. Moe felt a renewed sense of purpose, commitment, energy, and pride in the work, despite its drudgery.

ASK YOURSELF . . .

- In what ways do I feel that what I do makes a difference?
- What aspects of my work contribute to my sense of meaning?
- Work is a means to an end for most of us – what motivates me to work?

We have noticed four interconnected aspects of meaning that affect work fit (see Figure 3-1).

You Feel Seen – You bring something unique to your work.
Feeling seen means that the organization you join actually cares about you. Not the generic you, the person with the training and experience to simply fill the job, but the actual you, by name, with the unique synthesis of qualities and insights that will add unique value to the role. Our

human need to belong is tightly connected to our feeling seen at work. John, an engineer at a large solar inverter company, shared this painful experience of not feeling seen:

I started my new job full of hope and excitement. As a new engineering grad, I longed to make a difference by joining a renewable energy company. Within my first three months, I wrenched my back at work, meaning I was out for six weeks on disability leave. To my surprise, beyond the routine HR call about my return date, no one reached out to me when I was out. And even worse, when I came back to work, no one even seemed to notice that I had been gone. People on my team just assigned work as if it was my first day, no one asked how I was feeling, and I felt that the work I had started before I left had been completely abandoned. I knew then that I was just a cog in the wheel of essentially an engineering sweatshop. They didn't need me, with my unique ideas and value; they just needed someone (anyone) to crank out the formulas. I looked for a new job within days of my return.

Feeling seen doesn't always happen automatically. In addition to a genuine interest in you from others, there are things you can do to create more connection with other people at work, including your boss, that will help you feel seen and be seen. For example, try to practice sharing yourself openly at work with others. For private people this can feel challenging, but it's an important step to being seen and valued. Ask yourself, "What might other people want to know about me that would create more connection and, therefore, trust?" If you go first, others will often follow your lead and share about themselves in a more open fashion.

You Feel Necessary – What you do matters to someone and has an impact.

Do you remember your first job? For many of us it was during high school, when we were motivated by simply having pocket change to spend on our teenage interests. This first job often arrived accidentally and wasn't related to a cause we cared about. With little forethought as to whether our efforts mattered, we often caught on once things got going. Susan told us, "Serving coffee at a local shop near my high school, I grew to love the regulars. One customer told me, after a few weeks of coming in to sit at my table, that he loved seeing my smiling face. I learned that his wife had recently passed, and they used to come together to the shop.

I began to feel how wonderful it felt that to one person it mattered how I did my job because it brightened his day."

For many of the people we interviewed, the context of their work – the why – mattered more than we could have imagined. Oftentimes, you can shift how you feel about being necessary simply by understanding the context of your work, your boss, and your coworkers. Sometimes more research is needed to see how your daily tasks affect an actual human being. When Carletta worked as a billing training specialist at a cellular company, she felt demoralized by the work at times because it seemed difficult to convey to customer service agents why the billing system mattered. She asked to visit customers, and heard story after story of how the new billing system streamlined their understanding of costs related to the new technology and supported their buy-in to the actual costs of cellular to their business. Armed with the impact the system had on real people, she found it more energizing and compelling to train users on the system.

It's critical that you put energy into understanding the context of what you do and the impact it has on actual human beings or processes. Doing so increases your feeling of mattering to the end product or mission. If you don't understand the role you play, and to whom it matters, consider this exercise:

ASK YOURSELF . . .

- How would I describe the relevance of my role?
- Do I feel necessary? Why or why not?

You Feel Occupied – Engagement increases when you feel seen and necessary.

Engagement is a popular buzzword for organizations as a measure of the extent to which employees feel connected to and stimulated by the company they work for. Have you ever had a job where you watched the clock tick minute by minute? The odds are that if you said yes, you were marginally engaged at work. When we feel occupied, the time seems to fly by! And when we don't, we find ourselves surfing the web for job opportunities, fantasizing about better opportunities, and seeking make-work projects. Meaning is greatly elevated when we feel fully occupied by the work at hand.

There's much written about the role engagement plays in organizational success. But the role it plays for the individual is less frequently studied and considered. One of the things we do know is that when we feel only partially occupied by the work we do, we're functioning at less than full capacity. This dynamic means that, in many cases, we're not working to our full potential, and we leave talent, ideas, and innovation on the table. This contributes to us feeling increasingly invisible and unseen in our roles. As Barbara said about her work, "I know I could have brought more value to the job, but, frankly, I found myself mostly planning personal vacations in my head during down time at work. I would feel guilty, but I just couldn't find ways to think deeply about work – it mattered so little to me."

ASK YOURSELF . . .

- Do I feel proud when I talk about my company and job?
- What do I look forward to accomplishing at work?

You Feel Compelled – Your organization's products or mission are important to you; you can get behind them.

Increasingly, the element of meaning in work fit relates to the value, mission, and impact of the organization itself. Having a higher-order purpose – a contribution to the world, be it social, environmental, or simply producing an innovative product that makes lives better – draws employees who connect to that purpose and keeps them in the organization longer. Whether it's Starbucks' mission of "inspiring and nurturing the human spirit, one person, one cup, and one neighborhood at a time," Nike's mission of "bringing inspiration and innovation to every athlete in the world," or the Rocky Mountain Institute's vision of a world "verdant, thriving, and secure for all, forever," feeling good about why your employer and your job exist matters to us more and more. Sometimes it's not the mission of the organization that's compelling, but the nature of the role itself. Jill feels compelled; she said, "My job, even if small, is connected to larger social impact." Sinek (2009) speaks powerfully about this dynamic in his popular book and TED talk, *Start with Why*. He says "If you hire people just because they can do a job, they'll work for your money. But if you hire people who believe what you believe, they'll work for you with blood and sweat and tears."

Meaning matters to everyone at work, in every role. From factory work to C-suite, the ability to understand why your part at work matters is essential. Mario said it this way, "I know all I do is serve pizza. But people come in here tired after a long day and seeking a hot, delicious meal for comfort. They feel better when they leave, so I've done my job!" Barry Schwartz points out in his book *How We Work* the flaws in assuming either that a) only some jobs are actually meaningful or b) people will only want to work for a paycheck. He maintains that all jobs can compel human beings to strive, to sweat, and to risk.

Your Unique Purpose

Your purpose is not so much about *what* you do for work. It's more nuanced than that – it has to do with *how* you do your job and, even more importantly, *why*. Wrapped into your personal purpose at work are critical aspects of your identity, what makes you uniquely you. As Nick Craig and Scott Snook (2014) say in their article "From Purpose to Impact," "Although you may express your purpose in different ways in different contexts, it's what everyone close to you recognizes as uniquely you and would miss most if you were gone."

Reflecting back on your life to date, notice common threads and major themes. What consistently appears for you – lifelong interests, values, activities, and things that brought you pleasure? Go all the way back to childhood, before you had the pressures of what you should or shouldn't do. Think about the adversity or challenges you've faced and what techniques you used to navigate your way through them. Search for unifying threads and write them down. This exercise will help you to discern patterns and consistencies that may provide insight into the kinds of work that has brought you a sense of purpose throughout your life. Many of us have not thought about this aspect of work fit before, which may mean that we haven't examined what sense of purpose drives us. Looking for trends may provide clues to your own unique sense of purpose in your work, which is instrumental to finding great meaning fit in a job.

A software developer, Phil had been struggling with articulating what he felt his purpose was at work until he landed on the phrase, "I make complex things easier for average people to use at work." He was at times daunted by the endless coding facing him each week, but found new energy and hope by this simple articulated purpose. Phil used this as a type of mantra on a daily basis to focus his work.

Can you create a statement that expresses your purpose at work today?

Assess Your Meaning Fit

Intuition plays a huge role in our assessment of meaning fit at work. Spending time considering what it is that matters to you in the context of the impact of the work itself, the value your contribution has, the extent to which you'll be seen, or the compelling motivation for the organization's mission or purpose will assist you considerably in your search for an organization that satiates your human need for meaning. No matter what type of work you seek, pay attention to understanding what about the work or your part in it that makes you feel good and makes a difference and you'll be well on your way to satisfying your need for meaning. Use Checklist 3-1 as a reference as you progress in finding meaning fit and loving your job. We'll provide these checklists throughout this book to help you assess your work fit.

When it comes to loving your job, the meaning derived from doing it is an invisible, but critical, dimension of fit. In large and small ways, the context of the work you do and the meaning you derive from contributing provide deep satisfaction. All of us long to feel seen, necessary, occupied, and compelled. Sure, we can survive jobs where we lack feeling an inner purpose. But over the long term, our personal fulfillment is powerfully connected to our inner sense of purpose. Our work is one of the most fertile gardens for us to discover and cultivate ways to meet our basic human needs to contribute and to be seen.

ASSESS YOUR MEANING FIT ♡

☐ The things I care about also seem to matter to my company.

☐ I regularly feel sure that I'm contributing to something important.

☐ I'm clear about what I contribute.

☐ I'm satisfied that what I do makes a difference most of the time.

☐ My job taps into my interests and passions.

☐ I feel pride in working for this company.

Checklist 3-1. Check all of the statements above that apply to you. Use the checklist as a reference as you progress in finding meaning fit. You'll return to your answers in a final assessment of your work fit in Chapter 13.

CHAPTER 4

Job Fit

Everyone has been made for some particular work, and the desire for that work has been put in every heart.

— Rumi

WORKING AT A JOB that utilizes your gifts and leverages your knowledge creates wonderful feelings of contribution and satisfaction. It's that sweet sense of really being in your zone, doing what you do well and being acknowledged for it. We call this job fit. It happens when the responsibilities of your work align with your talents and provide opportunities for growth. A quote from one of our survey respondents sums it up well – she said that for her, job fit happened when "I was good at what I did, valued for it, and able to learn a lot."

Do you remember being asked when you were a kid, "What do you want to be when you grow up?" Our first toys – dolls, Legos, or art supplies – are often geared to helping us try out our future professions. Some of us dream of fighting fires, others of traveling in space or helping the sick. Over time, we start to differentiate. We may share our best friend's desire to be a pilot, but while her second choice is to be a marine biologist, we think being a chef is much more interesting. Only a few people will follow these early interests in a linear path; in fact, our career trajectories often appear quite random and rooted in circumstances. Nevertheless, our childhood dreams provide important clues about the job situations that truly make our hearts sing.

ASK YOURSELF . . .

- When I was a child, what did I want to be when I grew up?
- How did my childhood interests impact my path as an adult?

As we go through school, our interests start to intertwine with information on our aptitudes and talents. Teachers provide feedback on what we're "good at." For better or worse, these critiques impact how we view ourselves and how we envision our future. Are you a whiz at math? Perhaps a job in accounting is in store. Are your drawings always the ones that get featured in the school art show? Maybe you're headed for a career in graphic design. We move into adulthood and declare a major, start an apprenticeship, or land a first job responding to a combination of these interests and aptitudes as well as a variety of inputs from family and friends. For some of us, the perfect picture of job fit emerges early and stays consistent. For others, it's an ongoing journey of trial and error to return to the joy we experienced as kids role-playing our future desired profession.

Regardless of your stage in your career journey, finding the best job fit involves understanding and utilizing three factors – discovering your skills, gaining experience, and identifying your interests (see Figure 4-1).

Discovering Skills

Skills are foundational to job fit. You feel great when you can use your unique talents, abilities, and personal qualities to accomplish something and make a contribution to your company and to the world. As one survey respondent said about the importance of skills to her sense of fit, "Now I'm applying my professional skills in my specific professional area, and I have reached the top of my career. I'm very happy about this!"

Skills include areas such as written and verbal communication, planning and organizing, computer knowledge, and mechanical ability. Natural skill areas typically emerge early in our lives. Someone who loved standing up and doing oral reports in school is likely to exhibit the communication

Three Factors in Finding Great Job Fit

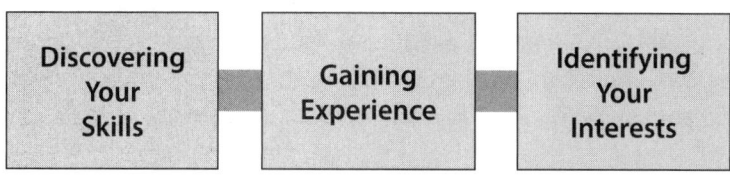

Figure 4-1. Regardless of where you are in your career journey, finding the best job fit involves understanding and utilizing three factors – skills, experience, and interests.

skills required to be a successful salesperson. An individual who constantly took apart and rebuilt things from their parents' garage is likely to have developed the mechanical skills that are necessary in engineering.

Skills may be directly related to functional job knowledge, such as a doctor's understanding of disease and appropriate treatments, or they may be indirect (or transferable), such as that same doctor's skill in communicating to patients or delegating tasks to staff. When considering your skills, it's critical to think about both your direct and indirect skills. Indirect skills like persuasion, organization, and leadership can transfer among many types of jobs and may be key to opening new opportunities. Most of us have a far broader spectrum of skills than we first acknowledge. For example, a computer programmer will have functional knowledge of a specific programming language that can easily transfer to a similar job in another company, but they will also have skills in areas such as problem solving and writing technical specifications that could be utilized in a vastly different job. Use the tool in Appendix 1, "Analyze Your Employability Skills," to assess your broad skills that are applicable to many kinds of jobs.

Our skills and preferences tend to lead us toward various occupations. Holland's (1997) theory of vocational choice provides one helpful model for mapping skills and personality types to possible careers. Holland groups individuals by one of six personality types: Realistic, Investigative, Artistic, Social, Enterprising, and Conventional. He then tracks each type to occupations that attract like-minded individuals. For example, individuals with realistic personalities gravitate toward activities that involve motor coordination, motor skills, and physical strength. They tend to prefer being physically involved in their work and might enjoy occupations such as electrician or aircraft controller. In contrast, individuals with social personalities gravitate toward activities that promote the health, education, and well-being of others, and they might enjoy work as teachers or psychologists. Appendix 2, "Holland's Six Occupation Types," presents a complete description of the six personality types.

ASK YOURSELF . . .

- What are my top three direct and indirect skills?
- What skills or traits do I think of as my personal superpowers??

Gaining Experience

Our natural skills are enhanced through education and experience. College classes, training, certification programs, and jobs can all play a role in developing and fine-tuning skills that contribute to job fit. A teacher with an education degree has built upon natural skills and gained the knowledge to control a classroom and prepare a lesson plan. By waiting on tables and working in the kitchen, a restaurant manager has gained the experience needed to ensure smooth operations throughout the restaurant.

Experience is related to the amount of time we've performed various jobs (more time equals more experience) and also to the particular events we've encountered. A young doctor who works in an urban hospital emergency room may have significantly more experience handling crisis situations than an older doctor with many years in a rural private practice.

For most of us, a strong sense of being valued for our skills and experience – our domain expertise – is a powerful component of job satisfaction. In many of our interviews, people lit up when they talked about a job where they felt uniquely capable to contribute.

Alison was hired to build a loyalty program for a new airline. She was brought in as an expert and liked being recognized for having a specific skill set that the company needed. "They were looking to me to lead the way in this area, which felt amazing. I loved being valued for my experience and knowledge and empowered to do what I do best." Her colleagues were also highly qualified in their individual areas. "Everyone had a special expertise and was operating at a very high level. We were all using our experience to make something great."

We work hard to build our knowledge through education and experience. It makes sense that we want to see it fully utilized and valued by our employers.

ASK YOURSELF . . .

- What experiences stand out as crucial to my growth in my career?
- What experiences have given me the most joy?

Identifying Interests

For a great job fit, you not only need the skills and experience to do the work but also genuine interest in the work itself. Confucius said, "Choose a job you love, and you will never have to work a day in your life." More recently, Steve Jobs (2005) echoed the idea by saying, "The only way to do great work is to love what you do." Sincere interest is one of the keys to great job fit; without it you may succeed but you won't thrive.

Such was the case with George. George showed an early aptitude for math. His father was an accountant and encouraged him to follow in his footsteps. "I didn't really get excited about my accounting classes in college, but I picked up the material pretty quickly and it seemed like a secure profession, so I declared it as my major, sat for the CPA exam, and began work for one of the big accounting firms. I'm a pretty social person, and it didn't take long for me to become frustrated by the many hours alone crunching numbers. I felt a little stuck because I had invested so many hours in training for the job. I wish I had thought more in college about how I might actually like the work."

As one friend noted about misfit, "I felt like I was doing what I was really good at . . . it just wasn't as gratifying as I hoped. What you're really good at doesn't always equate to what you enjoy doing."

When you have a job that aligns with your personal interests, it feels less like work. While we don't subscribe to the notion that if you simply do what you love, success will follow, we do believe that, when you genuinely enjoy or are passionate about the work you do, the work is less onerous and more interesting and stimulating. And the opposite is true as well. If you spend day after day doing work that bores you, it will ultimately show up in your performance and attitude. As one survey respondent said, "I'm passionate about my job, and it makes the long days fly by!"

For some individuals, interest in a job may be related to a personal passion. Chad loved his first job out of college working for a radio station because it connected him to his lifelong love of music. "Music was a big part of my life, and growing up this had been the coolest radio station in my town, so it was a dream come true to work there." The tasks and the pay mattered a lot less than the opportunity to interact with fans and bands and be part of a music scene. Chad knew it was "what I wanted to spend my life doing."

For others, interest is tied to a broader desire, such as leading, teaching, or solving difficult problems. Suzi, who works for a nonprofit, describes her job fit in this way: "I've been most content when working in civil service (teaching, nonprofit work, etc.) where my daily responsibilities were helping people. I just love doing jobs that directly result in building hope."

It's important to figure out the interests that will drive you to become the very best you can be. What are the activities that make you want to jump out of bed in the morning ready to take on the world? What are the things that will make you want to give 100 percent of yourself, rather than putting in the minimum requirement to pick up a paycheck?

ASK YOURSELF . . .

- When I've had a good day, what have I spent more time doing?
- If money wasn't a factor, how would I spend my time?
- How could I use my strengths and aptitudes in a way that would really feel good?

The Importance of Growth

Beyond matching your interests, experience, and skills, there's one other critical component that turns a good job fit into a great one – the opportunity for growth. In fact, in our research, the number one factor correlated to happiness at work was the opportunity for growth and development.

Conversely, lack of growth was a primary reason for people to leave their jobs. Sometimes that lack of growth happens over time, and opportunity just runs out. "While I had an excellent relationship with my boss and coworkers, I had gone as far as I could in the company, and no personal growth was in sight for the future. To grow I felt I needed to move on." On other occasions, it feels much more painful and personal. "My boss stifled my growth, didn't respect me, and was condescending toward her employees. Leaving the job felt like a breath of fresh air, a huge weight lifted off my shoulders, and a step in the right direction to pursuing my dreams."

Victor Lipman (2014), author of *The Type B Manager: Leading Successfully in a Type A World,* notes that "employees will always perform at their best when the environment is conducive to growth." He recognizes four different types of growth opportunities and notes that employees differ in which ones they see as most motivating.

- **Financial Growth** – Incentives preferably tied to employee performance

- **Career Growth** – Titles, added responsibilities, plusher offices, the respect of others in the organization . . . the various components of career advancement

- **Professional Growth** – The opportunity to improve skills and broaden knowledge

- **Personal Growth** – The more emotional aspects of life at work such as the opportunity to make new friends or receive recognition from peers

Along with being motivated by different sources of growth, we also have differing needs around the amount of "stretch opportunity" that's available to us. Some of us, like Michele, crave constant change and need jobs that are fast-paced and filled with new learning opportunities. She describes great fit as "drinking out of a fire hose and constantly diving into new challenges." Others just need a bit of variety to keep the day from getting wearisome. But all of us are wired for growth and personal development. All of us gain confidence and feel more fulfilled when we not only use our existing talents but are also able to develop new skills.

We believe that great job fit happens when we aren't so comfortable that we can do our job on autopilot, but where we aren't stressed in a way that erodes our confidence. One client described this as their zone of development – a place where they felt "mentally stimulated and challenged without being overwhelmed." Development may come informally through new job responsibilities or more formally through on-the-job training or mentorship. When we're in this zone we feel challenged, but the probability of success is good, and both the reward and the satisfaction are high.

For each of us, the balance between leveraging our current abilities and building new skills is highly personal. Our desired balance may change at different stages of our life and career, but the constant we see over time is that the ability to learn and grow is a crucial part of finding great job fit. As one survey respondent noted, "A wonderful fit is one in which you're challenged but supported, engaged but not overwhelmed. My current company has a culture that expects results but also expects its employees to grow and change over time. There are plentiful ways in which support and appreciation are shown, and the company provides the tools and resources for departments and individuals to perform at a high level. In an environment like this, knowing that I can aim higher and set stretch goals fills me with a willingness to innovate and think big. Regardless of whether my innovations or big thoughts could be implemented or are realistic or successful, just pursuing this level of envisioning what success looks like prepares me to grow professionally."

Daniel H. Pink (2009), author of five provocative bestselling books about the changing world of work, sums it up well by saying, "On days when workers have the sense they're making headway in their jobs, or when they receive support that helps them overcome obstacles, their emotions are most positive and their drive to succeed is at its peak."

ASK YOURSELF . . .

- When do I remember experiencing rewarding growth and development?
- What was the situation? How did it feel?
- What are areas where I would like to have more opportunity to grow?
- What's the right balance between comfort and stretch for me?

ASSESS YOUR JOB FIT

☐ My job is a good match for my skills, interests, training, and talents.

☐ I have opportunities at work to do what I really enjoy.

☐ My job makes good use of my previous experience.

☐ I have the right resources and support to perform my job.

☐ I feel that I'm learning and growing in my job.

☐ I have the credentials and education needed to do my job well.

Checklist 4-1. Check all of the statements above that apply to you. Use the checklist as a reference as you progress in finding job fit. You'll return to your answers in a final assessment of your work fit in Chapter 13.

Assess Your Job Fit

Once you understand which skills and experiences you want to use or further develop in your job, it's not difficult to assess job fit in your current work situation. Checklist 4-1 can provide a helpful framework.

If your checklist indicates that there are areas of opportunity to enhance your job fit, know that there are many strategies available to you to address it. We'll discuss these strategies in Chapter 15, "Flexing to Fit Where You Are." Job fit is also one of the easier elements of work fit to assess when you're evaluating new opportunities. Matching your job responsibilities to your skills, interest, and experience is critical to great job fit. It will be difficult to thrive if you don't feel able to perform well at your job even though you find it fulfilling and your organization provides opportunities for growth. So it's important that you and your job match. Finding that match takes persistence and courage, but it's possible to regain or create that sense of opportunity and excitement we felt as kids when we were role-playing future dream jobs. And the best part? Now we can get paid for doing it.

CHAPTER 5

Culture Fit

Customers will never love a company until the employees love it first.

— Simon Sinek

IN OUR OWN WORKING CAREERS and in our interviews we heard story after story of perfect jobs eroding into painful and frustrating relationships between employees and employers. Skills, experience, and interest feel perfectly aligned at first, then something else interferes with a job's capacity to bring out our best. Of the six critical elements of work fit, culture fit is often the hardest to grasp. It's largely invisible, unwritten, and unspoken, but, paradoxically, it causes employees the greatest pain, dissatisfaction, frustration, and failure to thrive.

While culture fit may be hard to grasp, when you get it right it's exhilarating for the employee and employer. Allie experienced poor culture fit at one organization because the processes were inconsistent and she felt unseen and undervalued. After moving on she found her sweet spot and experienced the joy that comes when the job fits right. She said, "I currently have a fabulous job. It's not the financial benefits – I've never made such a small salary. I help people; I'm valued. Relationships with service receivers and coworkers are valued and developed. There's zero micro-management (I feel tremendous trust for and from my boss and coworkers). I'm allowed creative freedom. I'm free to be my own person. *Mistake* isn't a word we use, only growth opportunities – and this is genuine. The culture comes from the boss, who truly doesn't sweat the small stuff and models calm and capable responses even in crisis."

In Allie's story we can see that how her new company does things aligns well with how she likes to work: she has freedom, mistakes are seen as opportunities, and the environment is stable. For Allie, these are the keys to culture fit. Two organizations in the same business may be very different in the environment they offer, and whether that environment works for a particular person depends on that person's preferences and needs. We can get a glimpse at the diverse views of what constitutes a good culture by looking at the ways CEOs describe their cultures:

> *Culture is simply a shared way of doing something with passion.*
> — Brian Chesky, Co-Founder, CEO, Airbnb

> *We try to have the kind of a culture that doesn't value excuses in the sense that when you're supposed to accomplish something, and you're at a high level, then your job is to accomplish it, in spite of difficulty. And you're rewarded for dealing with that.*
> — Phil Libin, Co-Founder, former CEO, Evernote

> *We have a culture where we are incredibly self-critical; we don't get comfortable with our success.*
> — Mark Parker, CEO, Nike

> *There's no magic formula for great company culture. The key is just to treat your staff how you would like to be treated.*
> — Richard Branson, Founder, Virgin Group

CEO's views are as diverse as a culture's effect on each employee. For Jasper, being treated by his boss the way his boss wants to be treated (as Richard Branson mentions) might appeal to his sense of fairness and equity, whereas Jane might be drawn to an accomplishment culture such as Nike's.

What is Culture?

Culture is often defined simply as "the way we do things here," and it profoundly impacts how we thrive at work. Jean described it this way:

"I couldn't put my finger around why the culture didn't work well for me at my first job. On the surface, it seemed ideal. But over time, it became clear that the way people acted with each other reflected beliefs and values that were inconsistent with what mattered to me. It came to a head when I noticed a pattern of senior leaders regularly presenting new ideas from their teams as their own. It just didn't sit well with me because it felt that the people doing the work were invisible."

People around the world have become very curious about culture and its role in organizations. With unemployment rates continuing to decrease to a low of 4.9 percent in October 2016 (compared to a high of 10 percent in October 2009) employees are increasingly in charge of determining where to work (U.S. Department of Labor 2016). Culture will remain a critical dimension in their choices and in their contentment with their choices.

Let's take a short moment to explain what we mean by culture, how it's measured, and its impact on work fit. By most measures, organizational culture matters to companies and employees for two key reasons:

- It determines the organization's ability to sustain its health over time via performance and results.

- It reflects an employee's daily behaviors, which determine ease of fit and probability of a long-term partnership.

Theories about culture gained popularity in business and management journals in the mid-1900s as organizational development (OD) grew as a field of research and practice dedicated to expanding the effectiveness of people within organizations.

Researchers suggested that organizational culture could significantly affect organizational outcomes, reasoning that culture could be used to affect employee actions, distinguish firms from one another, and create competitive advantage. Organizational cultures start with the values and actions of the company's founders and develop over time as the organization grows and responds to challenges.

Much press has been given in the past 20 years to company perks such as on-site day care, coffee lounges, dry cleaning services, and nap rooms, which we can think of as artifacts, or visible evidence, of culture. In our experience, these perks are far less important to employees than intangible rewards. Virgin Pulse's (2015) recent study showed that 77 percent of Millennial workers felt that culture was *more important* than salary and benefits. As Ray Hennessy (2016) said in *Entrepreneur* when he wrote about a company that offered to pay wedding costs as a benefit, "A company with a ping-pong table, ice cream socials, and all-expenses-paid Grub-Hub accounts can have lousy culture. Good company culture goes well beyond perks."

Over the last 65 years, as OD theory and practice have evolved, corporate culture has come into focus and is typically defined as the assumptions, values, and behaviors that contribute to the unique environment of a company. Often considered the father of organizational culture theory, Edward Schein maintained that culture was the hardest part of a company to change, outlasting products, services, founders, and all physical attributes.

Company values and beliefs are sometimes expressed formally in writing, but whether implicit or explicit, values become evident to employees during the course of work itself.

Cameron recalls a time when he realized that honesty was of primary importance at his new job. His boss, after the team missed a deadline, immediately called the client to inform them of the project schedule change and owned the problem fully. In other jobs, Cameron saw managers fudge to customers about deadlines and deflect accountability. He appreciated his leader staying true to the value of honesty. When your values are aligned with your company's values, it feels like you have a good culture fit.

Just below the values of a company lies the deepest level of organizational culture, the tacit assumptions held between the people who work there, often unseen and not consciously identified in interactions, but very much at play (Shein 1990, 112). These are what are sometimes called *the unwritten rules* of a company, and they explain why there can be paradoxical behaviors within an organization. For example, at a manufacturing company, despite its professed value that "People are the lifeblood of our company," senior leaders' decisions and actions reflected a higher value being placed on expense reduction than on people. When reward and recognition systems were designed and implemented, the company chose lower cost over employee retention, causing high turnover and low engagement.

It's that gap between professed values and tacit assumptions that often makes orientation and assimilation into a company a slow and arduous process for new employees.

Patsy says her situation felt ideal at first. After trying for several years to get hired by a public foundation doing great work, she was thrilled to get a program coordinator job and was relocated to a new city. At first, the culture fit felt great. The foundation's mission was a key driver for all activities, and people were energized and bought into solving big social problems together.

But after the first month, Patsy began to feel some rumblings of trouble. The organization was in a fast-growth mode and often scrambling for funding. This created high adaptability and flexibility, which Patsy appreciated. But she also needed clear and repeated processes. Part of Patsy's work style was to create order, organize, follow rules, and get similar results over and over again. As she learned the job, she realized that the organization was unpredictable and dynamically changing its basic processes. Over time, this created anxiety for Patsy, and after trying to make it work for more than a year, she realized that she needed a job with more structure and clarity so that she could really thrive.

ASK YOURSELF . . .

- What values do I cherish?
- How do my values affect my work?

Attributes of Culture Fit

When we examine cultural fit, it's important to differentiate between "a healthy culture" and "the right culture for me." But there are some characteristics that are seen consistently in organizations with generally healthy cultures, regardless of one's personal needs.

There are four attributes of culturally healthy organizations:

- Culture is discussed and examined at the very top.

- The organization has a viewpoint on moral and ethical behavior.

- Internal and external messages are consistent.

- The company embraces transparency.

In unhealthy cultures, these dimensions aren't present, or they're inconsistently applied, which creates stress, anxiety, and frustration for employees.

ASK YOURSELF . . .

- Does my current workplace possess these four attributes?
- If one or more are lacking, how important is that to me? Why or why not?

Once you know that these four attributes are in place, you can take a more in-depth look at the culture to determine how it aligns with your own personal values. (We'll discuss this in more detail in Chapter 12, "Knowing Yourself and What You Want.") For example, a company in a start-up mode is often focused on flexibility and customer responsiveness, whereas a manufacturer of consumer goods may emphasize extreme efficiency and consistency to drive lower costs. Most models and measurement tools that examine culture consider two primary dimensions: the way the organization responds to its external and internal environments, and the stability/flexibility it possesses. Figure 5-1 shows how Dan Denison and team depict this interplay of the two dimensions in examining culture. In addition to the two dimensions, their model features four organizational traits: Adaptability, Mission, Involvement, and Consistency. The bullet points below describe the characteristics of those traits.

Adaptability (external focus/flexible)

- The organization is able to learn.
- The organization is able to know and respond quickly to competitive innovations and customer expectations, as well as price.
- The organization invests in learning, training, and employee knowledge.
- Creativity and new ways to work are explored.
- Things are easy to change.
- Risk taking is rewarded.

Understanding Organizational Culture

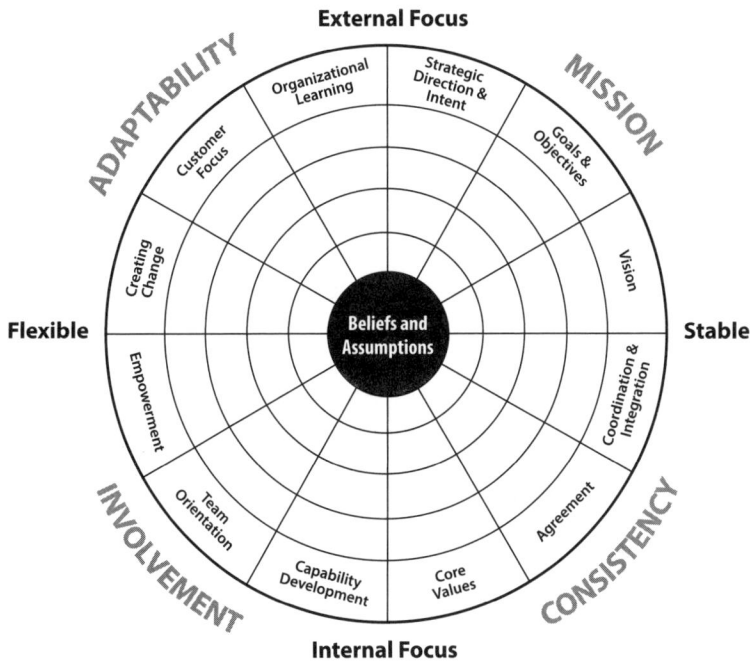

Figure 5-1. This graphic depicts the interplay of factors that affect the health of an organization's culture. The two dimensions of culture feature four organizational traits: adaptability, mission, involvement, and consistency. © Denison.

Mission (external focus/stable)

- Values are commonly understood.
- Clarity of "where we are going" and higher purpose exists for each and every role in the company.
- The organization has a long-term purpose and direction.
- There's agreement about goals throughout the organization.
- People know what must be done to succeed.

Involvement (internal focus/flexible)

- There's acceptance and appreciation for diversity.

- The organization displays a regard for and fair treatment of each employee as well as respect for each employee's contribution to the company.

- Employees show pride, engagement, and enthusiasm for the organization and the work performed.

- There's ample opportunity for each employee to learn and grow within the company.

- The organization has lower than average turnover rates (perpetuated by a healthy culture).

Consistency (internal focus/stable)

- The organization has consistent ways of doing things to get great results.

- There's a high degree of coordination and integration.

- Strong communication exists with all employees regarding processes, decisions, policies, and company issues.

- Aligned and transparent leaders possess a sense of direction and purpose; they walk the talk.

- The organization has one perspective and focus.

You can use the Denison model to help you assess a company's culture, which can be a bit of a detective exercise. Use these four organizational traits to help you categorize what you notice in the company you're assessing, and match the way the company works with how you like to work. When we first talked to Pep he said he knew that the company he was considering was a great fit for him from the beginning. Everything he saw resonated with him – how many bikes were stored in the commute locker, the friendly, calm way his future teammates greeted him, his boss's outfit, and the way the teams were organized. Pep loved being involved with others in his work and learning every day (Involvement). He instantly pictured himself as part of the company when he interviewed and felt at home from day one. Multiple small details about how they did things matched his style, which he described as "outdoorsy, active, informal, creative, and hardworking." Pep had felt burdened in a previous job by too many rules. He liked to work independently and really valued a flexible schedule (Involvement). When we talked to Pep a few years later he still felt that the company embodied the right culture for him.

In short, Pep thrived in an organization where he had a great deal of autonomy to do great work (Involvement). His creative orientation responded well when he had room to think without constant criticism, and where his unique, divergent views were seen as important and he was often asked what he thought (Adaptability).

ASK YOURSELF . . .

- How would I assess my company in terms of its internal and external focus?
- How would I assess my company on the stability/flexibility spectrum?

We suggest you consider two important caveats when looking for a great culture fit:

- In addition to the company culture, there's often a distinct work group or department culture that can be significantly different and also have a big impact on an employee working in that group. So consider the "local" as well as the overall culture of the organization.

- Describing a company as having a singular personality can be too narrow a parameter for a job seeker, since the essence of culture fit is complex, multi-faceted, historical, deeply personal, and dynamic.

Assess Your Culture Fit

Culture is one of the hardest elements of work fit to assess. You can feel that something is off but sometimes can't put your finger on it. A terrific culture to one person can feel incompatible to another depending on personal needs, desires, and motivations. When you assess culture fit,

ASSESS YOUR CULTURE FIT
☐ The organization's actions match its values.
☐ My communication style works well here.
☐ I feel fully engaged.
☐ I understand my role and my job.
☐ I am able to be myself.
☐ Processes are consistent and reliable.

Checklist 5-1. Check all of the statements above that apply to you. Use the checklist as a reference as you progress in finding culture fit. You'll return to your answers in a final assessment of your work fit in Chapter 13.

look below the surface – look at how people act. We act from what we believe, which is deeply rooted in our values and manifested in company culture. By paying attention to the nuanced, under-the-surface attributes of a company, and rigorously knowing the kind of environment that works well for you, you'll increase your likelihood of finding and thriving in a culture that's great for you.

When evaluating how your company's culture fits you, we suggest that you start with Checklist 5-1.

CHAPTER 6

Relationship Fit

The most important single ingredient in the formula of success is knowing how to get along with people.
— Theodore Roosevelt

LOVING THE PEOPLE YOU WORK WITH makes it a lot easier to love what you do. We have found that when people reflect on the work situations in which they felt the most connected, satisfied, seen, and engaged, a key element is the people. Clay, a senior leader at a global nonprofit think tank, said, "It's the people that make the hard parts of the job worth it. Despite some of my frustrations with the work here, or the stress, I come back every day eagerly because of my relationships with my colleagues. We're like a family."

Relationship fit is great when we like and respect the people we work with and when we receive the appropriate support and trust to do our job. Given how hard so many of us work to gather the skills, tools, and acumen to pursue a certain career, it can seem random and unpredictable to leave fulfillment at work in the hands of the random chance of finding people we can connect with easily in a job. So what exactly does it mean when we feel well connected to the people we work with?

What's Really Going on with Relationship Fit?

We form friendships over the course of our lives based on a variety of factors including simple association, proximity, shared interests, common goals and hopes, and galvanizing events. More important, however, are the characteristics of affection, empathy, honesty, trust, and compassion in the connections we make with people over time. In particular, we tend to feel friendship with those people whom we can most be ourselves with, making mistakes without judgment. This process starts in childhood and extends to school and, ultimately, to work. Tom Rath (2006), in his bestselling book *Vital Friends,* found that those who say they have no real friends at work have only a 1 in 12 chance of feeling engaged in their job. Conversely, if you have a "best friend at work" you're seven times more likely to feel engaged in your job.

We know from psychologists that love and belonging – in essence, friendship – exist as basic human needs for all of us (Maslow 1943). We require connection to others to feel whole.

It makes sense then that we carry these essential human needs for belonging and connection with us into the workplace, where most of us spend the majority of our time. Americans are working more than ever, often with two or more part-time jobs adding up to more than full time spent at work. With so much time spent at work, the connections matter.

Consider Christina's story: "As a working mother, when I'm not at work, I'm usually trying to spend time with my family. As a result, my non-work friendships have dwindled to non-existent. My work friends are important to me because we spend so much time together, and we're in the trenches, doing similar hard tasks every day. I don't know what I would do without them."

Most people form friendships at work in addition to friendships they may form outside of work (through childhood or family connections). When we start a job, it can feel wonderful just to experience shared interests and associations. Over time, however, the dimensions of relationships at work that grow to matter are more nuanced and harder to assess. These qualitative dimensions are often not evident until we're well into a job.

In particular, one element of relationship fit that matters the most to us is the presence of trust and respect by and with our peers. The ability we have to be fully ourselves with others, imperfect and authentic, but still accepted and welcomed, matters a great deal. In trusting relationships we can make mistakes, learn, and grow without fear of judgment or recrimination. In the workplace, the presence of trust between colleagues is a key element of team cohesion. Vulnerability-based trust matters the most in terms of feeling positively connected to people at work. Vulnerability-based trust forms when someone reveals a mistake, admits to not knowing something, or takes a risk without a promise of success.

The very dynamics of a workplace can often interrupt the formation of vulnerability-based trust. For example, workplace competition in which employees are pitted against each other, and only one wins, can eradicate trust. And ego or actions focused only on personal gain greatly erode the capacity of employees to build trust with one another at work.

Is There Trust in Your Work Situation?

There are several tells that indicate that a group of people have invested in creating positive and healthy trust-based relationships at work. Take a look at these common characteristics:

- Individuals talk openly about their strengths and their weaknesses.
- People offer both support and challenge in meetings, clarifying intention and asking questions without appearing judgmental.
- People know more about each other than just their names.
- There are references to people's lives outside the workplace (images, artwork, etc.).
- People seem to assume positive intention with one another.
- Competition is focused on winning in the market or against the competition rather than internally.
- Team leaders and people managers walk the talk.
- Talking to is balanced with listening to.
- People admit mistakes and discuss learning.

ASK YOURSELF . . .

- To what degree is trust present in my work environment?
- Do I feel that it's easy to show up as fully myself at work, or do I feel that I must leave parts of myself at home?
- Have I seen others admit mistakes freely?

When trust and respect don't exist between colleagues, the fit almost always feels bad. Politics, power mongering, competition, and subtle discounting behaviors degrade the faith and confidence of colleagues and create hidden and/or public tensions. Consider Mike's story of politics causing failed relationships at work. When he worked as the new COO of a turnaround manufacturing organization, Mike found himself consistently thwarted by one member of the leadership team who seemed unwilling to agree with any of Mike's ideas. Over time, Mike learned that she was strongly connected to the past COO and friends with many members of the board. Given this political dynamic, building buy-in and trust with her was a long and hard road.

In great fit situations, the evolution of healthy work relationships is proportional to the trust and mutual respect that's nurtured between people. We feel connected, so we feel safe, so we're willing to be vulnerable, so we courageously speak our truth, which elevates others' ability to trust us, and the cycle perpetuates itself. As Shelley said, "I knew I was valued and added value and my expertise was needed. I was in a friendly environment and enjoyed the people around me."

Conflict as a Good Thing

Another key dimension of healthy relationships at work is the ability to successfully navigate conflict. In dynamic workplaces, where people are innovating, creating, achieving results, and solving problems, they will inevitably disagree, have ideological differences, and confront divergent points of view. If left unresolved, these differences can stymie, stunt, and stop the work at hand. The ability of people at work to move from conflict to resolution is a key determinant of whether people feel great relationship fit.

Most of us don't eagerly seek conflict situations, since conflict tends to generate anxiety and stress. Nonetheless, the presence of healthy conflict at work allows us to feel good about the people with whom we work. Some essential elements present in conflict-healthy workplaces include:

- People challenge each other's ideas in meetings without hesitation.
- Issues are left on the table until resolved instead of being swept under the rug.
- When people disagree, it's done with respect.

- Conflicts are seen as ideological differences and learning opportunities rather than personal attacks.
- People tell the truth, even when it's hard.
- Bosses model healthy conflict with their colleagues and with their teams.
- There are no "meetings after meetings" because people are forthright with their feelings in a real-time way.

Paul describes his experience working in government for 20 years as often frustrating because people hesitated to disagree: "In government, people are terrified of making decisions because they'll be punished. People would rather do nothing than make a mistake, and they're rewarded for that." But to his delight, Paul and his current team members work hard to allow conflict and dissent between each other; in fact, they seek it, and he feels that this generates the best ideas. It took having a boss who was "not afraid to make a decision"; as a result "people tell each other what they really feel without fear of being punished for their input." He loves his job today and, in particular, appreciates that his team can disagree and still do great things together.

In seeking great relationship fit at work, it's wise to examine and understand your own capacity to build trust and mutual respect and to handle healthy conflict. Check out some of our tips in Chapter 12, "Knowing Yourself and What You Want."

ASK YOURSELF . . .

- The last time there was a conflict at work, how satisfied was I with the resolution?
- Do I spend time and energy actively avoiding situations at work where there may be disagreements?
- Do I feel listened to, even when I see things differently?

The All-Important Boss Relationship

All of us experience our company most directly through one lens: our immediate supervisor. No matter what title we have, the relationship that matters the most is, hands down, with our boss. Years of research confirm that the most common reason people quit a job is that they have a poor relationship with their boss. Even as peer-to-peer interactions grow in importance at work, the primacy of the boss relationship and its importance to us shouldn't be underestimated. In our interviews and survey, person after person commented that they left jobs, or felt stuck and unhappy, primarily because their relationship with their boss was poor. Carl said it this way, "I felt that I had an abusive boss/CEO who had the pretense of values but wasn't authentic. I grew tired of feeling unimportant, part of a machine." Or as Rachel said, "It was stressful to work for a manager who doesn't value you, in a culture of people who aren't invested in your development and contributions."

The relationship we seek with our boss is complex. In addition to being the primary way in which we experience the company, we depend on our boss for task assignments, information sharing, political navigation, feedback, resources, and clarity. At its best, a great boss relationship fit feels like working with a healthy mentor. They care about what happens to us, listen, and share themselves with us in an open and transparent way. Michelle described a great boss this way, "In a nutshell, I would lie down in front of traffic for him. I trusted John to have my back, to tell me the truth, and to both work hard and hold the big picture for all of us. I would love to work with him again anywhere, anytime." In contrast, a poor boss relationship fit stimulates the most unproductive behaviors possible at work. Distrust grows, feedback is withheld, mistakes are hidden, and backstabbing can prevail. At their worst, bad bosses don't walk their talk, don't make it their business to know their unique employees, don't listen, and take credit for other people's work.

Here's what you should look for in a great boss:

- Trust (vulnerability!)
- Transparency
- Time for you
- Support
- Competence
- Interest in you as an individual
- Constructive feedback

In addition, recent research by Benjamin Artz (2016) at the University of Wisconsin, Oshkosh, suggests that bosses' competence has "a significant measurable impact on a worker's satisfaction and overall well-being." In this study, supervisors' competence had more to do with employee happiness than other potent factors such as level of education, tenure, earnings, industry, and occupation.

At times, it's not the boss's lack of competence that irks you, but a profound difference in your styles and approaches. As Robin said, "It was disappointing to realize that a job for which I had held high hopes was a poor fit. I could tell almost immediately that I wasn't comfortable communicating with my boss; it was almost as though we weren't speaking the same language. Although I'm usually a high achiever, I found myself just trying to avoid interacting with him."

ASK YOURSELF . . .

- How do I (really) feel about my boss?
- Can I talk openly about most things?
- How do I interact with my boss?
- How does my boss give me feedback?

Remember that your relationship with your boss is a unique partnership. Kathy was caught off guard when Paul was brought in as her new direct boss. He was newly promoted to senior vice president, a position that hadn't existed before, and Kathy's former boss, a vice president who could have been developed for that role, took another job elsewhere. Their first meeting was off-putting. Kathy described the situation as "socially awkward, rushed, and impersonal" when she first met Paul as he was unpacking things in his office. Kathy was surprised that he didn't ask about her role or tenure with the company, but instead spent their whole 15-minute meeting telling her about his last job. She left the room longing for her previous boss and unsettled that she felt no positive connection with her new boss. But instead of overreacting, Kathy made it her business to learn more about Paul and to interact with him in as many ways as she could. She frequently invited him to coffee, checked in with him after meetings, and listened carefully when he assigned tasks. This took extra effort, and Paul's lack of curiosity about her concerned her, but she learned that his strategic direction was aligned with hers, and he seemed fair. Within a few months her attentiveness paid off. As Paul settled into his new job, he revealed that he had been very nervous since he really needed this job, and he felt a lot of internal pressure to perform well. He admitted that he hadn't been a good listener and asked her to let him know if he misstepped again because he was overly self-focused. His honesty and vulnerability impressed her, and she chose to share some of the concerns she had had about him at the beginning. With burgeoning trust their relationship became solid, open, and productive within six months.

Often there are things you can do to improve a poor boss relationship fit (short of changing bosses!). We suggest that you spend some time understanding your natural relationship strengths by reviewing Chapter 12, "Knowing Yourself and What You Want." In addition, explore ways that you can flex to fit a poor relationship with a boss in Chapter 15, "Flexing to Fit Where You Are." Self-awareness is the first step to a great boss relationship – knowing the kind of person you connect well with, and can be inspired by, will help you to determine where and how you can adapt. Then pay attention to how your boss operates, their style of communication, their work habits, and their skill at managing, which will help you to accurately assess the reasons that your boss is either a good fit or is bringing you down at work.

When to Go for Help

In some cases, relationships at work become seriously broken, damaging, or even toxic. If you find yourself in a situation where you feel scared or uncomfortable at work because of offensive behavior, intimidation, threats, or abuse by a coworker or superior, inform your HR representative. If there's a valid case for bringing charges of harassment, bullying, or workplace intimidation, it's critical that the behavior has been reported first. Poor work fit in the realm of relationship fit is very different from being harassed, and the two should be treated differently. If the situation isn't hostile, but is unproductive, a direct conversation with your boss can often ease the tension. If needed, HR or another manager can participate in support of a productive conversation.

Assess Your Relationship Fit

When we feel trust, respect, and rapport with the people we work with, we feel good about our motivation, engagement, and outlook. Writer, executive, and leader Margaret Heffernan (2015a) says, "Social connectedness plays a role in making individuals and companies more resilient, better able to do conflict well. Investing in the connections among team members both increases productivity and reduces risk."

Using Checklist 6-1 is a great start to looking at how the relationships in your current role are working for you. When you're working well with others, the work is easier.

Who we work with is as important as what work we do, if not more so. Our many years of consulting to and working within organizations

---

ASSESS YOUR RELATIONSHIP FIT

☐ My boss and I share similar work-related values and philosophies.

☐ I generally trust my boss and we communicate well with each other.

☐ I enjoy spending time with my coworkers.

☐ I feel respected and trust my coworkers.

☐ I have good friends at work.

☐ Conflict is healthy and productive here.

Checklist 6-1. Check all of the statements above that apply to you. Use the checklist as a reference as you progress in finding relationship fit. You'll return to your answers in a final assessment of your work fit in Chapter 13.

on issues of culture, leadership, teams, and strategy has shown us that the hard stuff is the soft stuff. What brings organizations to their knees is often not a failed strategy or a bad product but a breakdown, miscommunication, or conflict between people at work.

For example, chronic mistrust between sales and production may result in poor communication, low quality, and unhappy customers who buy less. Or an organization where employees are afraid to speak out about issues may pass defects along to the next stage, hiding mistakes. For people to bring out their best ideas and innovations, they need an environment of trust, respect, kindness, and empathy that enables courage and risk. In your quest for great work fit, spend time examining the relationships you're likely to form with your peers and your boss. It will make all the difference.

CHAPTER 7

Lifestyle Fit

Don't get so busy making a career that you forget to make a life.
— Dolly Parton

HOW MANY HATS DO YOU WEAR? Employee, parent, athlete, boss, artist, coach, caregiver, spouse, friend? We're wired with a spectrum of needs and desires that aren't met through just one role. We crave the acknowledgment and extrinsic rewards that come with a fulfilling job, while also desiring the companionship of family and close personal friends, or the deep sense of purpose that may be found in community service, travel, or a favorite hobby. As a result, we find ourselves constantly juggling. Every day we make hundreds of decisions about how to spend our time and energy. We navigate competing demands, expectations, and desires as we try to fulfill our many responsibilities without depriving ourselves and disappointing others. Lifestyle fit is about making this balancing act more manageable.

Great lifestyle fit happens when our priorities and responsibilities at home and in our community are in sync and supported by our job requirements and our employer's culture and policies. Our research and experience suggest that most of us struggle at some point with lifestyle fit and that, more than with any other element, lifestyle misfit can cause significant relationship, mental, and physical health strains. When meeting demands in one role makes it difficult to meet demands in others, you suffer. When these conflicting demands compete unsuccessfully for your finite time and emotional energy, your work and other relationships and responsibilities suffer as well.

ASK YOURSELF . . .

- What are some of the roles I currently play (parent, employee, boss, volunteer)?
- If you had to rank the roles in order of importance, what would that look like? Why?
- Do responsibilities in one role make it difficult to meet responsibilities in other roles?

If you feel a strain between your commitments at home and at work, you're not alone. In a study conducted by Barry Posner (2010), 50 percent of managers agreed with the statement "anxiety about my job frequently spills over into my home and personal life." In a 2010 study by researchers Danielle Talbot and Jon Billsberry (2010), 68 percent of the participants mentioned their families, other social networks and connections, or obligations they have in their communities as affecting their fit at work. Changing societal norms, such as the influx of women into the workforce, the increased prevalence of dual-earner couples, movement away from traditional gender-based roles, and technology that blurs the line between work and personal time, all contribute to the challenge. When you add factors such as the tremendous growth in the number of single parents and in employees taking care of aging relatives, lifestyle challenges affect all of us.

While the stress of competing obligations is increasing, our willingness to make extreme sacrifices for work is decreasing. As one respondent said, "In my best job ever, I had a lot of flexibility and had more work-life balance. I didn't have to take a hit at home." As companies realize this, norms, expectations, and practices are changing at work. For example, a drywall products manufacturing company implemented four-day workweeks for all employees during the recession and found that employees loved the schedule and wanted to keep it year-round.

Posner (2012) found that only 38 percent of managers in 2009 answered yes to the question, "Would you give up attending an important function at home if it conflicted with an important job-related function?" This represented a significant decrease from 1981, when the number was 60 percent. When asked, in 2009, "To further your career would you move your family to a new location for a higher paying and/or more responsible job?" 48 percent responded yes or probably and 36 percent said no or probably not. In 1981, 57 percent said yes or probably and only 25 percent said no or probably not. As we discussed in Chapter 9, the world of work is rapidly changing. Most people are no longer willing to blindly put work ahead of everything else in their lives. If you're struggling with lifestyle fit, you can take heart that companies are waking up to this new reality and more options are emerging. Achieving the right lifestyle balance is difficult but possible if you honestly consider your needs and the trade-offs you're willing to make.

Just How Important Is Work, Anyway?

Achieving great lifestyle fit begins with honestly assessing the various roles you play and the importance of work, at this particular moment, in your overall life and identity. In our experience, some people view work as necessary and even desirable, but of secondary importance to their other responsibilities. For these individuals, work isn't an end in itself but a means to acquire resources to enjoy other parts of their lives. This has led many workers, since the recession, to become contractors in their specialty fields, doing piecework through networked communities for a host of clients. The upsurge in on-demand workers in recent years, also called "gig economy workers," isn't showing any evidence of slowing down. Intuit estimates that, by 2020, the number of employees working this way will double (Sharpe 2016). The flexibility of on-demand jobs works well for many employees today from a lifestyle perspective, even though there are often elements lacking (such as predictable income, healthcare insurance, workers' compensation, etc.). There are many benefits to on-demand work, either for people seeking permanent flexibility and autonomy or as a stopgap for those in transition.

At the other end of the spectrum are individuals who get most of their identity needs met through job accomplishments and who see

The Lifestyle Fit Spectrum

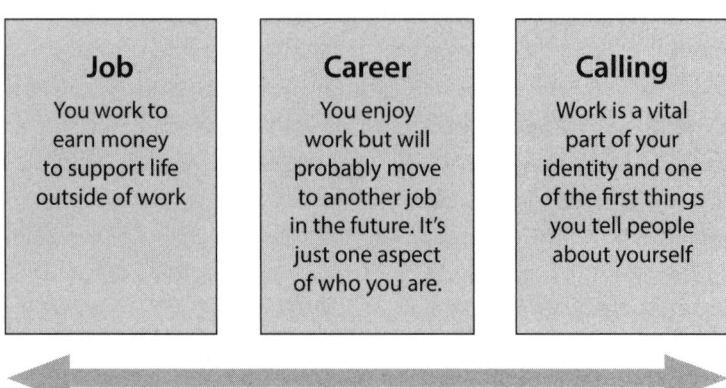

Job	Career	Calling
You work to earn money to support life outside of work	You enjoy work but will probably move to another job in the future. It's just one aspect of who you are.	Work is a vital part of your identity and one of the first things you tell people about yourself

Figure 7-1. To assess your lifestyle fit you need to first figure out where you are today on the lifestyle fit spectrum.

work as their first priority. Researcher Amy Wrzesniewski and colleagues (1997) categorize people into three groups: people who have jobs and are only interested in the material benefits from work; people with careers who have a deeper personal investment in their work and mark achievements not only through monetary gains but also through advancements within the occupational structure; and people for whom work is a calling, inseparable from the rest of their lives. None of these groups is better than the others. We may shift our perspective at various stages in our life; what's necessary for assessing your lifestyle fit is figuring out where you are today on the lifestyle fit spectrum shown in Figure 7-1.

We've seen individuals in what look like dream jobs struggle because they really wanted to spend much less time at work and much more time at home with their children or in pursuit of an outside vocation. And we've seen others in fantastic part-time, flexible situations grow frustrated because they really wanted the thrill and recognition that comes from being in a fast-paced, highly demanding job, or they longed for income predictability. Circumstances may intervene, causing you to put more or less focus on your work role than you want, but you may be able to improve your situation if you know what a great lifestyle fit would be for you.

ASK YOURSELF . . .

- How important is paid work relative to my other roles?
- Where do I get the greatest sense of accomplishment?
- Which roles give me the greatest sense of joy?
- What would be an optimal balance of my time and energy?

Your answers matter because they contain clues about the trade-offs you're willing to make and the areas you want to prioritize. A young father who wants to be actively involved with coaching his children's teams may choose a job that pays less but offers maximum flexibility. An aspiring CEO fresh out of business school may be thrilled with a consulting job that requires long hours and tremendous travel but also offers exposure to senior executives at multiple companies. Depending on your answers, you may find certain occupations or certain companies to be a better lifestyle fit.

Consider the case of Amazon. After a *New York Times* article detailed the allegedly family-unfriendly work conditions at Amazon, numerous employees came forward to say that they liked working in a company where the reward for hard work is even harder work (Kantor and Streitfeld 2015). They found the all-in experience of working with highly talented colleagues on challenging problems to be extremely rewarding. Other (mostly former) employees found the grueling hours, harsh judgment, and environment of "purposeful Darwinism" to be far more bruising than they could accept. This was especially true among some parents who said they left or were considering quitting because of pressure from bosses or peers to spend less time with their families.

Your needs and desires are unique. The right lifestyle fit for your colleague in the cubicle next door isn't necessarily the right fit for you. An employee working for Apple said it this way, "Everybody thinks this is my dream job, but I'm actively looking. Apple is a great company, but for me right now, the trade-offs are too great for my lifestyle."

Your lifestyle fit needs are dynamic – the importance of work relative to your other responsibilities will likely vary at different stages of your life. Your willingness to make significant lifestyle sacrifices may be different when you're just out of school and establishing a professional reputation (what we call Early Real Life) than when you're in your fifties and dealing with an aging parent (Maturing). We've heard many stories of individuals who felt that they had a great lifestyle fit at one point in their career and then struggled as their circumstances changed. We'll go into more detail about stages of life in Chapter 12, "Knowing Yourself and What You Need."

One of the most significant lifestyle changes comes with parenthood. Work conflicts tend to increase with the presence of children and can vary with their ages or individual needs. Greater family demands – more children or adult dependents at home – frequently create a need for more flexible or less-demanding work conditions. Job requirements you once embraced, such as weekend hours or extensive travel, can suddenly create significant stress.

In some cases, these demands might lead you to change your occupation to one with different requirements and greater flexibility. Leslie moved from high-profile, high-demand marketing jobs at Pepsi and Twentieth Century Fox to significantly greater flexibility as a university administrator. "My career move to higher education enabled me to enjoy a lot more control over my time. If I needed to take my son to the doctor, or if I wanted to attend a school function, it was easy to set aside my work and do it later at home."

In other cases, a lifestyle change might lead you to request a new role with your current employer. When her son was born, Cammie was heading up national sales for a major grocery manufacturer. Her customers and her team members were spread across the United States in eight different cities. "In sales, nothing replaces face-to-face interactions. Whenever I was in my home office in Dallas I felt like I was letting down my team and my customers. I felt a major conflict between what I knew I needed to do to be a good sales leader and my new role at home. I asked to move to a job that required much less travel. Because I had been a good performer with the company for many years, they were willing to make that accommodation."

While becoming a parent is a common reason for a change in lifestyle fit, it's certainly not the only trigger. John was a mid-distance runner in college who embarked on a career in high tech after graduation. He kept running for fun, and discovered, in his late 30s, a penchant for running ultra-marathons, sometimes over 100 miles. His job at the time was a nine-to-five office job, but he felt that to compete at the level he wanted to it would work best for him if he could flex his hours, allowing him to get long, multi-hour training runs in early in the day. Despite some trepidation, John approached his boss, and after some negotiation they agreed that he could try a flextime schedule that allowed him to come in at mid-day three days a week, working into the evening. His ability to pursue his passion elated him, and his running improved with a consistent, productive training schedule. At work he managed to schedule meetings with others during their overlapping hours. And his productivity increased because there was less distraction at the office in the late evenings. His employer was pleased with the result, as was John.

ASK YOURSELF . . .

- Has my lifestyle situation changed recently?
- If so, has this changed what I need from my job and my employer?

When considering the needs that arise from your roles, it's also critical to assess your level of outside support. The availability of family resources – parents who live close by or a spouse who isn't employed or works from home or part-time – can make a difference in the level of flexibility you require or the work conditions, such as travel, that you can successfully assume. Economic resources to purchase reliable and flexible child or elder care are another factor.

A growing lifestyle fit factor for many individuals is the amount of time it takes to commute to the job. When you're juggling multiple roles and every hour counts, time in traffic can cause stress and anxiety. One study conducted by Canada's University of Waterloo concluded that people with the longest commutes have the lowest overall satisfaction with life (Hilbrecht, Smale, and Mock 2014). The authors report that commute lengths are linked to a sense of time pressure. People who spend the most time on the road experience higher levels of stress because they constantly feel hurried. Many of them spend much of their time on the road worrying about all the activities they're missing. If you're seeking to prioritize outside-of-work responsibilities, your commute time may be a critical factor in lifestyle fit.

Work-Home Boundary Preferences

Another important component of lifestyle fit is the boundary between your personal life and work. Boundaries between work and home are blurring as portable digital technology makes it increasingly possible to work anywhere, anytime. Individuals differ in how they like to manage their time to meet work and outside responsibilities. Some people prefer to separate or segment roles so that boundary crossings are minimized. For example, these people might keep separate email accounts for work and family and try to conduct work at the workplace and take care of family matters only during breaks and non-work time. We've even noticed more of these "segmenters" carrying two phones – one for work and one for personal use.

Flexible schedules work well for these individuals because they enable greater distinction between time at work and time in other roles. Other individuals prefer integrating work and family roles all day long. This might entail constantly trading text messages with children from the office, or monitoring emails at home and on vacation, rather than returning to work to find hundreds of messages in their inbox.

Different jobs, cultures, and bosses have different norms around boundaries. Consider what works best for you and make those needs clear with your manager and work colleagues.

ASK YOURSELF . . .

- How much flexibility at work do I need to take care of outside responsibilities?
- What support can I count on?
- How much time does my commute take away from other, more-productive activities?
- How comfortable am I blurring the boundaries between work and home?

A Word on Gender Differences

While both men and women struggle with work-life conflicts, the challenges can feel different. Societal norms have given men and women different perceptions of their work and family roles. It's not unusual for men to feel that family interferes with work but not feel that work interferes with family. Working moms, on the other hand, often perceive that, not only does the work schedule interfere with their family time, but also that household responsibilities take away from the resources and energy they have to give at work. This isn't surprising, given that women still perform up to 19 more hours a week doing household tasks and devote on average 7 more hours a week to family then men do. Perhaps because of these pressures, 50 percent of women with children say that their ideal situation is to work part-time, compared to only 15 percent of men (Parker and Wang 2013b).

In addition, having a flexible work schedule is much more important to working mothers than it is to working fathers. Fully 70 percent of working moms with children under 18 say that having a flexible schedule is extremely important to them, while only about 48 percent of working fathers place the same level of importance on this.

Great lifestyle fit, however, isn't just a need for women. Research suggests that men are facing more emotional conflict than ever as they seek to spend more time on activities outside of work. The National Study of the Changing Workforce – a 30-year-long study from the Families and Work Institute – found that 60 percent of fathers reported experiencing work-family conflict in 2008, an increase from 35 percent of fathers in 1977 (Galinsky, Aumann, and Bond 2009). As Gary Barker says in the 2016 *State of America's Fathers* report, "Never before has the gap been so large between what parents of all genders want in terms of parental leave and support for their caregiving roles, and what our state and federal governments, workplaces, and social norms permit" (Heilman et al. 2016). And Erin Rehel and Emily Baxter (2015) add, "This rise in work-family conflict reported by men has grown alongside a new fathering ideal where being a good father means more than what some have termed 'earning as caring.'"

Attitudes are changing dramatically as Millennials become a more dominant force in the workplace. The Pew Research Center found that

Millennial fathers were more in favor of paid paternity leave than Generation Xer or Baby Boomer fathers: 93 percent of Millennials said it was somewhat, very, or extremely important, compared to 88 percent of Gen Xers and 77 percent of Baby Boomers (Parker and Wang, 2013a).

ASK YOURSELF . . .

- Do I face unique challenges based on my gender, race, or any other difference?

- How could my work change in a way that would be more supportive of my needs?

Assess Your Lifestyle Fit

Now that you've reflected on your current lifestyle fit requirements, you can more clearly assess whether your current job and organization are providing the support that you need. Checklist 7-1 is a good place to start.

If the checklist highlights that lifestyle fit is an issue for you, don't lose heart! More organizations are recognizing that employees need to contribute at work and also fulfill outside responsibilities, and they're increasingly implementing practices that allow employees to satisfy those needs.

Some level of tension between your many life roles is to be expected. Every day is filled with trade-offs and decisions. But success in one role shouldn't mean undue sacrifices in other responsibilities that are important to you and bring you joy. With honest reflection on your needs, and proper due diligence in assessing the organization's policies and norms, you can find great lifestyle fit. And when you find it, the good feelings you have about one role are likely to boost your confidence and self-esteem in others.

In Chapter 15, "Flexing to Fit Where You Are," we'll provide you tips on how to negotiate a better lifestyle fit with your current employer. If that's not possible, in Chapter 17, "Evaluating New Opportunities," we'll provide you ways to assess your lifestyle fit in a new opportunity.

ASSESS YOUR LIFESTYLE FIT 🏠

☐ I feel that I have the right balance between my job and time outside of work.

☐ I find my work challenging but not overwhelming.

☐ There isn't pressure to work long hours that interferes with my life outside of work.

☐ I feel that I can meet my personal and family needs while also working productively.

☐ My job is flexible in the ways I need it to be.

☐ Travel to and from work is convenient.

Checklist 7-1. Check all of the statements above that apply to you. Use the checklist as a reference as you progress in finding lifestyle fit. You'll return to your answers in a final assessment of your work fit in Chapter 13.

CHAPTER 8

Financial Fit

Some people are so poor; all they have is money.
— Patrick Meagher

WHILE YOUR PAY is one of the most visible and seemingly concrete components of your work, the role of financial fit is more complex and requires deep reflection on both your current and future needs. Your financial compensation not only involves your base pay, raises, bonuses, and commissions but also additional currencies such as vacation time, healthcare benefits, and opportunities to save for retirement. Your needs are multi-faceted – some are practical, such as understanding the cash flow required to take care of financial obligations, and some are more closely tied to identity and emotional desires. Financial fit is great when all of those needs and realities match your employer's compensation currencies. Like the other work-fit elements, financial fit isn't static, and it must be considered in the context of those other elements and your stage in life.

While compensation frequently plays a large role in whether you decide to take a particular job, it has a relatively small role in ongoing work fit. In our research, compensation was actually ranked lower than job content, relationships, and culture as a reason why people see their work as a great fit. We hear repeatedly from people who say that they love their job so much they would take less pay if necessary, as well as from people who find that high compensation can't make up for lack of fit in other areas. A study by Glassdoor found that an employee's compensation and benefits rating had the second smallest effect on overall satisfaction (Nuñez 2015). The only thing less important to employees was their company's business outlook rating. In research by Deloitte, 95 percent of job candidates said that culture is more important than compensation (Bersin 2015).

Nancy had this to say about the role of financial fit compared to other elements: "I had a really good position with solid compensation and stability, yet I wasn't allowed to develop professionally in ways that fit my strengths, so I quit that job for a part-time position. It was the best decision ever! Great people to work with and an amazing training opportunity for me – at this point in life those things matter more to me than the extra income."

Of course, this doesn't mean that you should work for free or simply follow your bliss and hope that you'll have enough money to make ends meet. It's unwise and naïve to assume that money doesn't matter. There are many hard-working people who struggle mightily to ensure that they're able to pay their bills and provide for their families. Insuring that your basic needs are covered is critical and foundational to thriving in any capacity. Not being able to meet your financial obligations is an obvious sign of misfit, but once basic needs for food, shelter, transportation, and clothing for you and your family are met, the psychological benefits of money tend to diminish.

In a widely cited paper, Daniel Kahneman and Angus Deaton (2010) reported that in the United States emotional well-being levels increase with salary levels up to a salary of $75,000 – but that they plateau above that. While the actual dollar level may vary depending upon where you live and work – $75,000 buys a lot less in San Francisco than in Kansas City – the point is an important one. Once your basic needs are met, more compensation by itself will typically not result in a better work fit or increase your sense of thriving.

Felt Fair Pay

What *does* matter to financial fit is a sense of fairness. Given the amount of time and energy you devote to work, you want to ensure that you're valued in an appropriate way. This is called felt fair pay. Receiving less than you need or deserve can lead to dissatisfaction that can impact commitment and, in some cases, confidence. So, while great financial fit won't guarantee success or happiness, poor financial fit is likely to cause harm and stress. As one survey respondent noted, feeling unfairly compensated led to "anger and bitterness." Another respondent called it "stressful and frustrating" to be undervalued financially.

Pay equity has become a hot topic for organizations and individuals. Unlike the past, where social taboo made it difficult to compare your pay with that of other people, today there's a general move toward greater transparency, with multiple resources available to find standard pay rates. Many women and minorities still face tremendous pay gap issues. Controlling for factors such as career level, education, skills, job responsibilities, and more, researchers at PayScale (2015) have found that women earn between 3 percent and 5 percent less than men for equivalent work. For some industries, such as finance and tech, the gap is much higher. And we've encountered numerous clients – male and female – who have found that after years with the same company they were being paid less than newer hires.

An important way to ensure that your pay is fair is to be proactive in knowing what your skills are worth. Grounding yourself in the facts can be especially critical if, like some men and many women, you're not comfortable or experienced in negotiating for more pay. Salary.com found that 84 percent of employers expect prospective employees to negotiate salary during the interview stage (Gouveia 2013). Yet only 30 percent of women negotiate, while 46 percent of men do (Babcock and Laschever 2007).

You can use websites such as payscale.com or glassdoor.com to compare your salary to those in similar jobs, factoring in location, experience, education, and other attributes. Once you gain this knowledge, you'll be better equipped to negotiate with your current employer or decide to move to a job that provides a better financial match.

ASK YOURSELF . . .

- How am I being compensated relative to averages for my profession, location, education, and level of experience?

Knowing Your Cash Flow Needs

Understanding what you need for great financial fit requires a realistic assessment of your expenses. It's important to consider all annual, quarterly, and monthly expenses. This includes your rent or mortgage, car payments, car insurance, credit cards with outstanding balances, gym memberships, entertainment, hobbies, family obligations, and grocery bills. If you don't know that number, get out a piece of paper and figure it out. Once you know your total annual expenses, calculate what that is monthly. To understand your financial options, it's critical to have a good grasp of your obligations and spending patterns.

Rich was unhappy in his job as a software engineer, and he decided to accept a position to do web development for a nonprofit where he had been serving as a volunteer. The change meant a significant decrease in salary and therefore a big decrease in spending. "I've had to make sacrifices, but it's worth it. Now I help people, I'm valued, I feel tremendous trust from my boss and coworkers."

Like Rich, you may want to take a job that pays less but provides great fit in other areas. To do that you have to figure out how to spend less each month. You may also have to save money and reduce your debt prior to making the job switch.

While there will be a minimum threshold you require for monthly pay, the way you prefer your compensation to be structured can vary tremendously based on factors such as family situation, stage of life, and personality. Your need for a pay structure that's fixed vs. variable, or short-term vs. long-term, can be a critical part of establishing great financial fit.

For example, an individual with fewer outside financial commitments, perhaps someone who's single with no children or someone who has a partner with a steady, dependable income, may be quite comfortable with pay that's highly variable. Variable pay can be great but risky. A real estate agent or a salesperson who's heavily commissioned may make a large income one year and significantly less the following year. This can still be a good fit if your fixed financial obligations are low or if you have other sources to turn to in lean times.

Similarly, some financial compensation packages are focused on short-term value (base pay and bonus) while others are structured around long-term incentives (equity, retirement savings plans). As with variable pay, the more certainty you need to meet daily financial obligations, the more you may trade off potential long-term gains. This willingness to prioritize short-term pay over future potential will vary based on your current financial situation, your projected needs for the future, and how close that future is. For example, someone with little savings who has children nearing college age may be less likely to bet on less salary and the potential for long-term gain than someone in their early twenties.

Don't forget, your pay package is only part of the equation. Your total compensation may include benefits such as health insurance, dental/vision benefits, vacation time, personal days, disability insurance, and perks such as free food and gym facilities. Even factors such as job title or access to training programs can provide great value over time. Smart organizations are increasingly designing their compensation programs in the context of a total rewards strategy that takes into account pay, benefits, and non-monetary rewards such as career paths and work-life balance. Each of these has different value to different individuals. Know what's most important to you.

Jamie worked in patient collections at a large community hospital. A single mother, she had average health insurance and didn't think much about coverage at first. Over the years, however, as first one and then both of her sons developed health concerns requiring frequent medical treatment and intervention, health insurance became key to how she felt about her financial fit. She had taken a new job with a higher salary, but left it after a few months to join her previous employer, who offered full medical coverage for all employees, including their dependents. As the medical bills mounted, having comprehensive coverage was far more important to Jamie than a higher salary.

The Psychology of Pay

Beyond meeting functional needs, financial fit may also be tied to your psychological needs. This is different from the tangible compensation we just discussed and is closely tied to identity, and it can have a major impact on your sense of being fairly valued. People differ in their view of money and the role it plays in their identity.

For some individuals, money represents an important symbol of power and achievement. Dan lived in Silicon Valley and had seen many of his peers make money on stock options when their companies went public. He felt left behind as they moved to nicer neighborhoods and bought expensive cars. So he left a secure job for a role in a smaller company that was primed to go public, in hopes that he too would be able to hit the jackpot. It was worth the risk for Dan.

For others, money represents a means to future security. Lori stayed in a job she grew to dislike because staying longer meant hitting certain retirement savings milestones – more savings meant more freedom for her and her husband once they stopped working.

Money from work may be a way to support other passions. Nick valued the flexibility of contract work because he could choose to work more or fewer hours based on his financial needs of the moment. His preferred lifestyle was to work a contract for six months and then travel for six months.

You need to understand what financial compensation really means to you. The pursuit of power, recognition, status, security, family support, flexibility – these are all legitimate financial motivations. The role that money plays in motivating you will shape what you look for in an organization and its compensation package, and it will certainly shape how you balance financial fit with the other elements of work fit.

ASK YOURSELF . . .

- Do I know what I need to earn in order to meet my financial obligations?
- What is my preferred mix of fixed vs. variable compensation? Short-term vs. long-term?
- What benefits are most important to me?
- Are there other psychological needs my compensation should address?

Assess Your Financial Fit

You deserve to be paid fairly based on your experience and on what's typical for the position. You need to be compensated in a way that enables you to meet your obligations and fulfills larger psychological needs. Checklist 8-1 can help you understand just how well your current situation meets your needs.

ASSESS YOUR FINANCIAL FIT $

☐ I feel that my pay is fair.

☐ I appreciate my overall compensation package, long- and short-term.

☐ There's a good match between my job and my pay.

☐ There's a good match between my job and my benefits.

☐ I can take care of my responsibilities with what I'm paid.

☐ There's room for growth in my pay over time.

Checklist 8-1. Check all of the statements above that apply to you. Use the checklist as a reference as you progress in finding financial fit. You'll return to your answers in a final assessment of your work fit in Chapter 13.

If you've identified areas of misfit, Chapter 15, "Flexing to Fit Where You Are," will provide tips to help you negotiate a better financial situation with your current employer, while Chapter 17, "Evaluating New Opportunities," will help ensure that any new opportunities are a better match. It's important to remember that financial fit interacts with the other elements of work fit in significant ways. Perhaps just as important as your total compensation are intangible benefits such as the opportunity to develop new skills, access to talented mentors, the chance to relocate to a desirable area, a culture that feels like home, or adding a prestigious company to your resume. Great fit in areas such as job content or lifestyle may increase your comfort with less compensation. On the other hand, you may want higher pay to make up for less-desirable attributes of the job. In Chapter 13, "Calculating the Elements and Weighing Trade-Offs," we'll show you how to consider financial fit together with the other elements of work fit so that they all add up to you loving your work.

PART III

WHY FIT MATTERS

CHAPTER 9

The Changing World
of Work

*There's always a story. It's all stories, really. The sun coming up
every day is a story. Everything's got a story in it. Change the
story, change the world.*

— Terry Pratchett

THE STORY OF WORK IN AMERICA today isn't pretty. Workers are feeling overwhelmed, burned out, disengaged, anxious, and stressed out to the point of feeling ill. People are working more hours than ever, especially in competitive professions such as law and management, and many people report feeling pressure to work even more than the 47-hour-a-week average reported by Gallup (Saad 2014). Despite studies that show that our collective health, wellness, and performance are decreasing with long hours, people are working even harder and taking fewer vacations for fear that if they don't appear "all in" they may lose their jobs. In their article on managing high-intensity workplaces, Erin Reid and Lakshmi Ramarajan (2016) said that "organizations pressure employees to become what sociologists have called ideal workers: people totally dedicated to their jobs and always on call. . . . In such places, any suggestion of meaningful outside interests and commitments can signal a lack of fitness for the job."

Human beings at work are simply not thriving, and this affects the performance of the organizations in which they work and the communities in which they live. Despite technological and social gains worldwide, the people who do the daily work tasks to keep economies, industries, and governments contributing are less vibrant, happy, and fulfilled than ever before, and they're therefore likely not doing their best work. The traditional "good jobs" supported by Roosevelt's New Deal, which offered good benefits, permanent security, and potential for advancement, have evaporated under the weight of startups, mergers, and global connectivity.

Michael graduated from a good university a few years ago with a bachelor's degree and a great GPA. After studying leadership, he decided to work for a few years before deciding if grad school was right for him. Six months as an office worker left him empty and demoralized because of the drudgery and sameness of the work. Next, he worked at a factory on a bread line, hoping that manual labor would provide some satisfaction. A tri-lingual speaker, Michael is passionate about climate change and corporate responsibility; he's frustrated that he hasn't been able to find a place to hang his hat, but he doesn't want a corporate job with endless hours. He wonders, doesn't anyone want a worker like him? Someone who wants to make a difference, can work hard, can write well, and is very good on a team? He'll give his all to the right job if he can find one!

Joan, on the other hand, is in her early 50s and considering her next move. She studied accounting as an undergrad and has worked hard her whole career as a mid-level finance person. Her kids are almost grown, and she would love to find work that makes her heart sing a bit more. She's had three bosses in three years and wonders if there's a better role or company for someone like her. She worries that her computer skills are dated, but oh how she would love a change!

Joan and Michael, in two very different stages of life, seek jobs that will fulfill them and put bread on the table, but they're struggling to find the right fit. They're not alone: a study by The Energy Project found that 59 percent of workers are physically depleted, emotionally drained, mentally distracted, and lacking in meaning and purpose. In the same study, only 30 percent of employees say they have an opportunity to do what they enjoy most at work (Schwartz and Porath 2014b).

Key Factors to Deteriorating Happiness at Work

The world of work is in great flux. There are new productivity tools introduced every week that are supposed to help us get more work done, faster. We're connected with employees and colleagues worldwide via a

Workforce Trends that Impact Fit

1. New and Ambiguous Roles

2. Increase in the Desire for Meaning at Work

3. Flexibility as a Currency

4. Information Overload

5. Distributed Companies and Teams

6. Speed

7. Cloud Workers (Outsourcing)

8. Sustainability Imperative

9. Diversity

10. Overwhelmed Workers

11. Generational Turnover

Figure 9-1. Listed above are the top trends affecting employer/employee fit today.

multitude of devices that are always on. These changes in the world of work have both positive and negative effects on people globally.

Let's look at the top trends affecting employer-employee fit today:

New and Ambiguous Roles

New jobs appear every year that didn't previously exist, with titles such as Social Media Coordinator, Director of First Impressions, Unschooling Counselor, and Growth Hacker, to name a few. In our technology-driven economy of service businesses, where information (data) rules, jobs are morphing in novel and unanticipated ways. Gone are the days when the selection of one career path in a known profession was a sure thing for life (doctor, lawyer, civil servant). And even in known professions, paths are changing quickly. For example, physicians may review MRIs from thousands of miles away without seeing the patients, or marketing managers may work only in the digital media realm. And this pace of change will increase over time – it's estimated that 65 percent of the jobs that will be available when today's kindergartners graduate college don't even exist today (Rosen 2011).

Increase in the Desire for Meaning at Work

The days when a job was just to make money to provide for the family have passed; the purpose behind our drive to work has shifted. Increasingly, new workers (especially the Millennial generation) seek meaning when they look for a job. This means that despite the perks, promotions, pathways, or professions of a particular role, if employees can't find a higher purpose in their work or company, they'll feel disconnected, disenfranchised, and, ultimately, misfit (see Chapter 3, "Meaning Fit"). While it's possible that this has always been so, it feels more acute today when long-term employer-employee relationships are not a given. In fact, most people can expect to have 11 to 13 jobs during their lifetime.

Flexibility as a Currency

Workers today aren't satisfied with traditional nine-to-five work hours and much prefer to schedule their work around hobbies, caregiving, and lifestyle choices. This alters the traditional construct of an "office" where people sit in cubicles or meeting rooms and crank out documents and information. People want portability and flexibility regarding the way they work.

Information Overload

Today, availability of data isn't an issue: we're swimming in information every minute of the day, accessible by various devices and from locations as wide-ranging as a boat in the Arctic to our neighborhood Starbucks. Access to information isn't an issue, it's knowing what information to pay attention to, and whether that information is relevant to our decision-making process.

Distributed Companies and Teams

Digital connection anywhere, anytime, means that people and work are no longer organized in traditional settings. People work across platforms, time zones, languages, and cultures more than ever before, putting increased demand on communication, clarity, and team cohesion. This trend puts pressure on employees at all levels to build social capital with people in all directions to get things done. It's not only feasible but likely that you have a boss or teammates you've never met in person. This changes how we relate to one another, how we partner, and how we learn.

Speed

Things happen faster than ever in the world of work, resulting in increasing pressure for workers to assimilate huge volumes of data and make decisions fast for fear of falling behind or missing an opportunity. The internalized pressure to do more in less time leads to the iconic heads down, shoulders hunched, running-in-place image of U.S. workers – all action, very little reflection.

Cloud Workers (Outsourcing)

An increasing number of workers are freelancers today, and companies frequently reduce costs by outsourcing work to part-time or occasional workers to avoid overhead (Nunberg 2016). This combination provides flexibility for workers but fails to deliver stability and predictability, which impacts their ability to keep ahead of living expenses, plan for major life events, and take advantage of company benefits. This trend has negative implications for the social contract between employer and employee regarding long-term security, and this affects families, communities, and individuals.

Sustainability Imperative

Business growth for growth's sake is being replaced by many organizations with purposeful profitability – responsible growth done in ways that minimize impact on the environment, people, and communities – where greed has given way to values, profit with impact, and business as a force for good. The rise of social entrepreneurship means that more and more companies form daily that not only make money but also make a difference. The new business status of benefit corporations and B Corps (see bcorporation.net) – embraced by strong consumer brands such as Patagonia, Dansko, and Method – are evidence of consumers' interest in products that, at a minimum, do no harm. This has implications for employees, particularly given their increasing desire to find meaning and purpose at work.

Diversity

Numerous factors impact the extent to which organizations seek more diverse pools of workers. The case has been made that having people with diverse experience, views, and contributions makes companies better (as long as they can navigate conflict). Beyond quotas and government regulations regarding equal employment opportunity, organizations increasingly seek workers who represent their client population. And rather than focus on people who are alike, employers are seeking those with diverse experiences and perspectives to elevate their creativity and innovation. There are still challenges with recruitment and retention of minorities, but the tide has turned when it comes to an interest in and commitment to diversity.

Overwhelmed Workers

The volume and speed of changes in global markets have created an overwhelmed workforce. Because of this feeling of being overloaded, inundated, and overstretched, there's been a tremendous increase in the popularity of yoga, meditation, and mindfulness. Brigid Schulte (2014) writes in her book, *Overwhelm: How to Work, Love, and Play When No One Has the Time,* about the costs of our work-hard culture as well as ideas for how we can reclaim our lives together. With productivity decreasing with excessive work, we should all be incented to reduce or eliminate our feelings of being overwhelmed.

Generational Turnover

The long-anticipated brain drain of baby boomers entering retirement has hit at last. With an estimated 53.5 million Millennials in the workforce in America in 2015, the transfer of power and influence is well underway, and because of generational differences we'll undoubtedly continue to change how we work. Millennial workers are motivated by different priorities and are, by their very nature, changing how work unfolds. Interestingly, a 2015 Gallup survey showed that Millennials are the least-engaged generation at work – only 28.9 percent say they are actively engaged (Adkins 2015).

ASK YOURSELF . . .

- How have I been impacted by any of these workforce trends?

- Are there other trends that are impacting my work situation?

Impact on Our Fit

So what do these trends mean in terms of your ability to find the right work fit?

What We Look For In A Job Has Shifted

Let go of outdated notions of what to look for in a job. Gone are the days when incremental salary increases, a desk with a view, a particular title, and prestige were essential elements of work. In the new world of work, what matters to us is dramatically different, and we have more leverage than ever before with employers to get exactly what we want. Smart companies know that it benefits them to find workers who are a good fit, so knowing what matters to you significantly increases the likelihood of finding a great fit.

The Six Elements of Work Fit, Reprioritized

The six elements of work fit that we've identified are likely very similar to those that mattered to employees in the past, but the importance of each element has shifted, especially since the global recession of 2007–2009. Meaning and lifestyle fit, for example, have become more important as employees let go of traditional notions of the American Dream, such as financial gain, and focus instead on their well-being.

Culture fit has become increasingly vital to a workforce that values transparency, which is much more available in the digital age of social media; employee empowerment initiatives and studies have shown that the ability to feel like you're a part of the company greatly increase motivation and morale.

Job fit has shifted since many entry-level jobs require advanced education, and people are specializing with more training and experience. And, finally, relationship fit shows up in the work-fit equation because people increasingly work as part of multiple teams, requiring unprecedented partnership and collaboration.

The Process is Highly Personal and Subjective

The proliferation of "Great Places to Work" rankings in magazines reflects the degree to which employers care about their company being perceived as a favorable workplace. And to a degree, these ratings and company descriptions are useful to job seekers, helping them to find companies whose employees rated certain attributes highly. On the whole, though, our research confirms that just because a company is on the list doesn't mean that they're the right fit for you. In fact, because of their time sensitivity and focus on morale and motivation, these ratings function best as promotional tools for an organization rather than as a provider of any guidance for you in determining potential work fit. Time after time, we've interviewed employees who worked in top "Great Places to Work" who left because the work fit was poor for them.

Learning Matters

In the face of today's dynamic workplace, the opportunity to learn and develop in a role, at any level, is extremely important. Our interest in growing, in contributing, and in learning more (about the work, ourselves, the organization, the market, being a team player, and leading) is a critical aspect of finding an ideal work fit. Because we'll hold many jobs over our lifetimes, one of our essential human needs – to get better by learning and growing – can and should be met by our work.

Society Needs Organizations, So Fit Matters

Despite the growth in the number of freelancers, there are still vastly more people employed full- or part-time by organizations. Our social structure depends on organizations large and small for some of the things that make civilization as we know it work: a tax basis that supports social services, retirement possibilities, insurance cost reduction, and the synergistic lift that organizations can achieve through cost sharing, innovation, creativity, and impact. Accordingly, if organizations continue to be the primary employers, work fit becomes essential to the organizations themselves as well as to the individuals who work in them.

It's Up to You

Companies are focused more than ever before on solving the puzzles of attracting and retaining the talent they need for their businesses to thrive, but ultimately the responsibility for finding a great work fit is on your shoulders. Knowing yourself, and being able to assess an organization for fit before you join it, are critical skills as you hunt for the right place to hang your hat. We expect that organizations will strive to get better at being people-centered to ensure fit and reduce their costs, but you, the individual job seeker wanting a great work fit, must take the reins and be responsible for finding the best workplace for you.

CHAPTER 10

How Fit Impacts People

Half of our waking lives is a terrible thing to waste.

— Barry Schwartz

IT'S A SIMPLE AND POWERFUL TRUTH: how we earn our living impacts far more than our bank account. Work shapes how we define ourselves and greatly influences how much we enjoy our lives. From our earliest years, we role-play future careers as firefighters, teachers, and construction workers. We spend years in school preparing for future professions. As adults, the first question we're likely to ask a new acquaintance is, "So what do you do?" When we lose a job, even one we didn't particularly enjoy, it strikes deeply at our sense of identity. Conversely, when we find a job we love, we gain joy and confidence, which spills over into other parts of our lives. Work is fundamental to our lives, and what we need from our work is, ultimately, more than a paycheck.

Given how much time we spend there, it's no surprise that our work is so intertwined with our self-image and emotional health. During a typical weekday, we spend more time working then we do sleeping and far more time than we spend eating, pursuing leisure or household activities, or caring for others (U.S. Department of Labor 2014). We spend almost as many hours a week with work colleagues as we do with family and far more than we do with friends. When we feel good about how we spend our time at work we thrive, but if work is dull or painful, if we feel unengaged or experience low trust, we're drained and inevitably suffer. Our friend Christina describes her work life this way:

"Work misfit was like a slow, inexorable slide into a deep, gray blah. I felt like something was wrong with me. How can I be earning so much money and still be so miserable? Why am I pouring liquor into my leftover coffee while I sit in non-moving traffic on my way home each day? Is this normal? Does everyone feel this way? Can this really be life?"

While we may recognize a general feeling of discontent, many of us fail to realize just how deeply work satisfaction and fit can impact our physical and emotional health. We convince ourselves that our circumstances are normal, or that we just have to keep trudging through them. We don't like to think of ourselves as quitters. Certainly there are times when sticking with a difficult situation can teach us resilience and help us to develop new skills, but it's critical to be aware of hitting that point where the pain far outweighs any gain.

Krista experienced the pain of misfit in her job at a large Internet company. "It was traumatic. While I was in the job, I tried working harder, but no amount of time was enough. I would become depressed on Sunday nights as I dreaded going back to work on Monday. It seemed that nothing I did was quite right and I could never satisfy my stakeholders or myself. It really messed with my self-confidence. I felt as though I was failing and blamed myself. I spent a lot of time afterwards wondering why it didn't work, what I had done wrong, etc. Even though it was my decision to leave, I felt the sense of not having been successful for a long time afterwards. It's only after working to better understand my strengths that I can see that it was a fit problem instead of a personal failing."

Misfit and The Work Cycle of Doom

In our research we've heard Krista's story play out time and time again. Misfit and the ensuing crisis of confidence frequently lead to what we call the work cycle of doom. When you feel unhappy at work you typically find it more difficult to motivate yourself, which often results in lower productivity. When you don't like your job, every molehill looks like a mountain. It becomes difficult to fix any problem without agonizing over it or complaining about it first. This is usually noticed by colleagues and peers. When you feel angry or resentful about your circumstances, it typically creeps through into your attitude and behaviors, with symptoms

Figure 10-1. The work cycle of doom is the flip side of the virtuous work cycle (see Figure 1-3).

such as low energy, passive-aggressive reactions, and lack of teamwork. This leads to negative feedback, criticism, and lack of support, which create even stronger feelings of misfit. Essentially, this work cycle of doom is the flip side of the virtuous work cycle described in Chapter 1, "Understanding Fit" (see Figure 1-3).

One of our survey respondents discusses her own cycle of doom: "The misfit affected everything: my level of engagement, my desire for professional growth, my relationship with my coworkers, my personal life. With little to no guidance and just an emphasis on doing my current job with fewer and fewer resources and support, I had to do my own professional development, growth, and networking. Obviously, doing that on my own led me to pursue other jobs. Leaving the job and my old team was a difficult decision, but it was the right one."

Lack of fit doesn't always result in needing to leave. Even in the face of misfit, it's possible to achieve work goals and develop positive relationships with hard work and deliberate actions. But these achievements are extremely difficult to attain and the effort typically creates significant stress. We've observed people who, despite misfit, kept up strong performance at work only to find that they were paying a significant price in other areas of their lives.

ASK YOURSELF . . .

- Can I recall a time when I entered a cycle of doom at work?
- What were the circumstances?
- How did I feel?
- How did I perform?

Work Fit Impacts Those We Care About Most

When our performance and emotions suffer at work, we frequently try to compartmentalize. Essentially, we say to ourselves, "I don't like my job but I'll just keep that separate from the rest of my life." This is possible for some people, some of the time. As we'll discuss in Chapter 15, "Flexing to Fit Where You Are," investing time in enriching activities outside of work can be a strategy for handling a misfit situation. Unfortunately, this tends to be a short-term solution. Just as in the proverbial story about the person who gets kicked at work only to go home and kick the dog, it's difficult to put away bad feelings when we leave the office, and it's even harder if we've spent all day at work hiding our unhappiness.

Typically, unhappiness at work spreads like wildfire, carrying over to our other activities and our other relationships. When most of our time is spent doing something that brings us down, or when we don't feel appreciated for the work we're doing, it's difficult to leave that pain at the office.

Deborah took a job at an established company to manage a new team that was formed mostly of employees from a recent acquisition. She was really excited about having the chance to fully leverage her experience in online marketing and customer relationships to make a big difference in the business. "Most of my team was in Denmark, and I was in California. I underestimated how difficult that would be. I was traveling all the time, and when I was at home my meetings all started at 7 a.m. To compensate I just kept trying harder. The stress took a high toll on my health and my family life. Feeling unhappy and uncomfortable at work, I was constantly trying to change myself to fit in while also feeling hopeless that it could ever get better. It was physically and emotionally exhausting. One Sunday night, as I was leaving for yet another overseas trip, my husband said, 'You are miserable and you are making us miserable.' I had not wanted to admit how much my lack of fit was impacting my family. I had eleven hours on the plane to think about it, and pretty soon after I quit the job."

When we're unhappy at work, our frustration and bitterness unconsciously seep into conversations with the people to whom we're closest. We need a place to vent these difficult emotions, but "you won't believe what my boss did this time" becomes dull if it's always the main topic. On the other hand, some people work hard to shelter friends and family from any suggestion that work isn't going well, only to slowly feel frustrated that they can't share their true emotions.

Friends and family want us to experience joy. They want to see us valued for what we do best. When work is going well, they celebrate with us, and when it's going poorly, they suffer as well. We can typically see this and give the right advice if a friend or spouse is in a misfit situation, but it's often more difficult to acknowledge it in ourselves. One marketing executive we interviewed said that when she's struggling with misfit, she steps back and considers what advice she would give her daughter if she were the one dealing with the situation. This exercise helps her to gain perspective on her situation and consider her options.

ASK YOURSELF . . .

- How does work fit affect my relationships with friends and family?
- When work isn't going well, what's the impact?
- If I'm struggling with misfit, what advice would I give to a friend in a similar situation?

Fit Impacts Our Health

One of the greatest long-term risks of staying in a job that doesn't fit is the impact it may have on your health. Numerous studies validate the significant relationship between work, stress, and health. Simply put, if you're in an ongoing work situation that's negative or stressful, you're more likely to suffer health problems. Even moderate amounts of stress can cause body pain, difficulty sleeping, and weight gain. High stress contributes to anxiety and depression, serious conditions that undermine daily functioning and health. Studies suggest that individuals who don't like their jobs are more prone to getting sick, even contracting serious ailments such as ulcers, cancer, and diabetes.

A decade-long research study of work culture, work-life fit, and health, funded by the National Institutes of Health, found that workers in supportive, flexible environments show half the risk of cardiovascular disease, significantly lower levels of stress, higher job satisfaction, and better physical and mental health (Work, Family and Health Network 2015). They sleep and exercise more, they're more likely to go to a doctor if they're sick, and they spend more time with their children. While we hope and believe that many employers are waking up to the importance of helping employees manage the levels of stress in their jobs, it will ultimately be up to you to recognize what's happening with your health and seek the changes needed to improve or protect it.

Steve experienced the impact that job stress and misfit can have on health in a dramatic way. When his small solar startup was acquired by a larger organization, it seemed like the capstone of his successful career and an opportunity for accessing greater resources for his team and their products. What he found was that he had landed in a cold, impersonal culture focused solely on profits. He was expected to lay off dozens of loyal employees and was publicly criticized by management for speaking honestly about issues. Because he had a lucrative retention contract he endured as well as he could – navigating between trying to stay true to his core values while being forced to implement decisions he vehemently opposed. The day his contract expired he quit, excited to finally spend time with his family. Instead he found himself barely able to get out of bed, incapacitated by mood swings and low energy. He was eventually diagnosed with a thyroid problem caused by chronic stress, and he's still in therapy dealing with post-traumatic stress disorder. "At work I was like a warrior putting on my armor every day. I was under so much stress for so long. What I failed to realize is that I would pay such a high price. I'll be paying it for a long time to come."

Good health is a powerful force in our ability to fully enjoy life. Like many things, it's something we frequently take for granted until it's threatened. We certainly can't enjoy our work if we're constantly battling aches and pains or feeling tired or anxious. We may not always connect the dots between misfit and the costs of medication, therapy, work-related injuries, and alcoholism, but those costs are very real.

ASK YOURSELF . . .

- If work is a misfit, what costs am I paying?
- What are those costs to my relationships, confidence, health, energy, self-esteem, and sleep?

Over the course of our working lives, we'll all face situations where we don't love our jobs. In some instances, it may be temporary, or it may be remedied by small changes. But if we lack motivation week after week, we need to make a change. In our research, those experiencing deep misfit described their situations as disheartening, demoralizing, agonizing, and stressful. These words represent real pain and real cost. The psychological impact of poor performance reviews, the toll of anxiety, depression, or poor health, are likely to come at a far greater cost than the paycheck we're putting in the bank. When we minimize these impacts, we denigrate our own well-being. "I'm sacrificing my life for that company" should be unacceptable to us.

CHAPTER 11

How Fit Impacts Organizations

Engaging the hearts, minds, and hands of talent is the most
sustainable source of competitive advantage.

— Greg Harris, Quantum Workplace

ORGANIZATIONS ARE WAKING UP to the recognition that work fit matters. They may use different words to describe it (employee engagement, employee satisfaction, culture, climate, or organizational health), but there's clearly a growing understanding that the better employees' needs are met at work, the healthier, happier, more engaged, productive, and loyal they are to their organization. People who enjoy their jobs are more likely to feel inspired by the goals and values of their company, exert effort, and stay employed with the organization. The business case is irrefutable – take care of employees and they'll take care of business.

The days when employees expected nothing more than a paycheck are gone. Led by Millennials, employees are increasingly seeking meaning as much as financial incentives from their employers and are unabashedly and rapidly changing jobs when their needs aren't met. As Barry Schwartz (2015), author of *Why We Work*, says, "We want work that is challenging and engaging, that enables us to exercise some discretion and control over what we do, and that provides us opportunities to learn and grow. We want to work with colleagues we like and respect and with supervisors who like and respect us. Most of all, we want work that is meaningful – that makes a difference to other people and thus ennobles us in at least some small way."

CEOs are responding to the trends and to the growing body of research in unprecedented ways. Mark Bertolini of Aetna raised wages, improved health benefits, and introduced yoga and mindfulness training. Netflix announced unlimited paternity leave. Google is legendary for its onsite amenities, which include a community garden, sleep pods, and cafeterias that serve free lunch and dinner. Leaders are paying attention to growing their capacity for fluently handling "the soft stuff" – motivating, inspiring, and connecting with the people who work for them.

Lara Harding, People Programs Manager at Google, said, "At Google, we know that health, family, and well-being are an important aspect of Googlers' lives. We have also noticed that employees who are happy . . . demonstrate increased motivation. . . . [We] . . . work to ensure that Google is . . . an emotionally healthy place to work" (Gourlay, 2009).

Franchise company Great Harvest Bread employee Bonnie Harry says, "Giving your employees space to learn and support to grow creates a symbiotic relationship. They gain valuable life and work skills and you gain not only good employees but also the satisfaction of mentoring and helping them. And if they move to another career, you've both benefited from the experience of working together."

In addition to gaining loyalty through perks such as updated offices, free food, fitness centers, and classes, smart companies are focusing on benefits to provide employees with more flexibility as well as looking for ways to get them involved in company decisions. Outdoor products retailer REI uses social media to get employees at all levels talking to each other via campfire circles about the things they care about (Kowalsky 2012). And small tech company TechSoft 3D involves employees in all locations in annual discussions on values and strategy to increase buy-in on where the company is heading.

Companies of all sizes are beginning to recognize that fit matters. Small companies reap the benefits of positive employee work fit even more directly than large companies since each person has a greater influence on morale and results. Employees at small and midsize firms often find opportunities to take on more responsibilities, earn greater recognition for successes, gain ample exposure to new practice areas, and have a more direct impact on a company's bottom line.

Employees want to be in an environment where their values and beliefs are aligned with the organization and where they feel supported to do their best work. In research among employees who were considering a job change or who had recently switched employers, the top reason for a change was that the employees desired an opportunity to do what they do best (Mann and McCarville 2015). They want to fully contribute their talent and experience. Employees desire fit.

So Just What Does Fit Mean to Organizations?

As we said in the first chapter, work fit isn't about looking alike or being part of the same social group, class, race, or gender. It's about employees having a common set of values, desires, and expectations with their organizations that allows them to do their best.

One commonly measured output of fit is employee engagement, typically defined as the emotional commitment an employee has to the organization and its goals. Emotional commitment means that engaged employees care about their work and their company. They don't work just for a paycheck, or just for the next promotion, but on behalf of the organization's goals. We believe that when fit is right the connection can go even beyond engagement to inspiration. Eric Garton (2015) at Bain & Company researched the difference between satisfaction, engagement, and inspiration. He found that if satisfied employees are productive at an index level of 100, then engaged employees produce at 144, nearly half again as much. But then comes the real kicker: inspired employees score 225 on this scale. From a purely quantitative perspective, in other words, it would take two and a quarter satisfied employees to generate the same output as one inspired employee.

As one pundit put it, employees react differently when they encounter a wall. Satisfied employees hold a meeting to discuss what to do about walls. Engaged employees begin looking around for ladders to scale the wall. Inspired employees break right through it. Inspiration happens when fit is right.

One of the first researchers to study organization-people fit was Jennifer Chatman (1991), a professor at Northwestern University. She conducted research over a two-and-a-half-year period in partnership with eight of the largest U.S. public accounting firms. She surveyed junior audit staff during their initial orientation, asking them to sort through value statements (about quality, respect for individuals, flexibility, risk taking, etc.) and rank how consistent each statement was with their own beliefs. After 12 months she had the junior auditors rate their satisfaction and intent to leave. She saw a high correlation between fit at entry and satisfaction, as well as a negative correlation between fit and intent to leave. In other words, when fit is good, employees are likely to contribute their best work, and companies obviously benefit from this.

Brian Chesky, CEO at AirBnB, understands this. Most companies create their core values after they've hired a few dozen people; Airbnb created theirs before they hired anyone. Before hiring his first employee, Chesky ran through hundreds of applicants and interviewed dozens of people. It took him six months to find the person who was the right fit. Chesky says that he viewed bringing in this first employee as analogous to bringing the right DNA into the company. He didn't view the process as merely bringing in a person to build a few features, he viewed it as a long-term investment in establishing the culture of the company. He wanted a diversity of backgrounds and experience, but he didn't want diversity of values. As Brian says, "There's no such thing as a good or bad culture; it's either a strong or weak culture. And a good culture for somebody else may not be a good culture for you" (Bulygo 2015).

Innovative companies strive to hire for fit but understand that they can't always get it right. Zappos believes so strongly in the concept of fit that the company offers exit payments to new employees who come to understand the organization and then decide that they're not a good fit. Zappos recognizes the tremendous benefits that come with the right match of skills, values, and goals, and the huge cost of getting it wrong.

The organizational costs of having employees who are misfit are significant. Gallup estimates that actively disengaged employees cost the United States $450 to $550 billion in lost productivity per year (Borysenko 2015). And the problem is global. Unengaged employees in the United Kingdom cost their companies US$64.8 billion a year. In Japan, where only 9 percent of the workforce is engaged, lost productivity is estimated to be US$232 billion each year. A bad hire costs a company revenue, customers, and productivity, in addition to the hard costs of recruiting, training, and developing a new employee (as much as $50,000 in the United States), and the costs increase the longer a misfit employee is on the job (Gallup 2013). Getting fit right from the beginning, or at least ending poor work fit sooner, saves energy, time, money, and effort. Let's look at some of the drivers of the cost of misfit.

Turnover

One of the easiest costs for organizations to quantify is employee turnover. When employees feel unmotivated and unhappy, they are much more likely to leave their job and employer. Turnover, both that which is initiated by the employee and that which is initiated by the company, has become a tremendous and troubling expense for organizations.

Because of differences in job complexity and skill levels, it's tough to say precisely how much value an employer loses when a worker leaves. Turnover costs also vary by wage and the role of the employee, but in all cases it adds up to significant expense. A Center for American Progress study found that the average cost to replace an employee is 16 percent of the annual salary of those holding high-turnover, low-paying jobs and up to 213 percent of the annual salary of highly educated executives (Boushey and Glynn 2012).

And these costs may fail to include a full accounting of the impact. Josh Bersin (2013), a consultant who has spent years studying the subject, outlines factors a business should consider in calculating the real cost of losing an employee. These include:

- The cost of hiring the new employee, including advertising, interviewing, screening, and hiring.

- The cost of on-boarding the new person, including training and management time.

- Lost productivity: it may take the new employee one to two years to reach the productivity of an experienced person.

- Lost engagement: employees who see high turnover among coworkers tend to disengage and lose productivity.

- Customer service and errors: new employees take longer to perform a task and are often less adept at solving problems.

- Training cost: over two to three years a business is likely to invest 10 to 20 percent of the employee's salary in training.

Beyond the detriment to the bottom line, turnover can damage team dynamics. The group loses not only rapport but the leaving employee's unique expertise and contributions. Teams must also shoulder the burden of extra work until a replacement can be trained. Furthermore, losing talented, knowledgeable employees can be a drain on a company's leadership pipeline, and rampant attrition can also take a toll on an organization's carefully cultivated workplace culture. The dynamics of the organization, such as trust between employees, the degree to which conflict can be navigated, and clarity of purpose and direction, change every time an employee exits or enters.

The evidence is conclusive – to avoid the high costs and disruption of turnover, companies need to do a better job of insuring that hires are a good match for the requirements of the job and the culture of the organization. As employee tenure continues to shift from people who work at one place for 25 to 35 years to people changing jobs 11 times or more in their lifetime, employers will feel pressure to speed up recruitment and orientation processes to reduce the costs of turnover, but these costs will still exist in one form or another.

Absenteeism and Lost Productivity

Even if they don't leave, employees who are misfit are likely to create significant costs because of their absenteeism. When they're suffering from job misfit, employees are likely to miss more days of work. While injuries, illness, and medical appointments are the most commonly reported reasons for missing work, they are not always the actual reasons. In our experience, there are many other factors that cause employees to "call in sick."

- **Bullying and Harassment** – Employees who are bullied or harassed by coworkers and/or bosses are more likely to call in sick to avoid the situation.

- **Burnout, Stress, and Low Morale** – Heavy workloads, stressful meetings or presentations, and feelings of being unappreciated can cause employees to avoid going into work. Personal stress (outside of work) can lead to absenteeism.

- **Childcare and Eldercare** – Employees may be forced to miss work in order to stay home and take care of a child or elder when normal arrangements have fallen through (for example, a sick caregiver or a snow day at school) or if a child or elder is sick.

- **Depression** – The National Institute of Mental Health asserts that the leading cause of absenteeism in the United States is depression. Depression can lead to substance abuse if people turn to drugs or alcohol to self-medicate their pain or anxiety. A study in 2010 indicated that depression caused $51.5 billion in indirect workplace costs because of absenteeism and "presenteeism" (reduced productivity while at work due to depression) (Robison 2010).

- **Disengagement** – Employees who aren't committed to their jobs, coworkers, and/or the company are more likely to miss work simply because they have no motivation to go.

Absenteeism costs U.S. companies billions of dollars each year in lost productivity, wages, poor quality of goods and services, and excess management time. According to *Absenteeism: The Bottom-Line Killer*, a publication of workforce solution company Circadian (2005), unscheduled absenteeism costs roughly $3,600 per year for each hourly worker and $2,650 per year for salaried employees. In addition, the employees who do show up to work are often burdened with extra duties and responsibilities, which can lead to feelings of frustration and a decline in morale.

Service, Quality, and Safety

The benefits of fit extend to the way that employees create products and deliver services. Research has shown that positive employees do a better job producing quality products and creating satisfied customers. Conversely, it's easy to imagine the potential outcomes from unhappy employees interacting with customers, making key decisions about quality, or evaluating product innovations. Poor quality, suboptimal manufacturing, and lost customers and revenue are all significant risks in such instances. A study by the consulting firm Denison tested the relationship between organizational culture and customer satisfaction using business-unit data from two different companies – a home-building company with multiple divisions and an automobile company with 148 dealerships. With a few exceptions, firms with higher culture scores had higher customer satisfaction ratings (Gillespie et al. 2007).

One positive example of the link between fit and service comes from Morrison Management Specialists, a company of more than 20,000 people that provides food, nutrition, and dining services to healthcare and senior living communities. Morrison recognized that their employees were the key assets and resources that would differentiate them from their competition. They undertook a number of activities, such as using virtual coaches and stay interviews (one-on-one conversations that reveal important ways to engage associates) to integrate talent-focused behaviors into the organization's culture and subsequently increase employee engagement, decrease employee turnover, and improve overall operational effectiveness. Major organizational metrics were tracked from 2006 to 2010, including employee engagement, turnover rates, and patient or client satisfaction. Employee engagement rose approximately 30 percent, turnover rates dropped approximately 15 percent, and client satisfaction rates rose approximately 16 percent, an important outcome. "We have no other significant change to tie this metric change to except that we are doing this engagement initiative," said Andrea Seidl, senior vice president at Morrison.

Similarly, at Saks Fifth Avenue, the luxury retailer based in New York, executives were looking for ways to boost service to customers in their highly competitive market. Saks officials decided to measure employee engagement and customer engagement at stores. Customer engagement included the willingness to make repeat purchases and recommend the store to friends.

Saks found that "there absolutely is a correlation between employee engagement and customer engagement" and that employee engagement creates loyal, repeat customers and increased sales (Bates 2004). Vice President Jay Redman indicated a 20 to 25 percent improvement in stores with great engagement.

A similar dynamic holds true for manufacturing firms. Companies with highly engaged workforces realize fewer quality defects, fewer safety incidents, and less waste. Beer manufacturer Molson Coors found that engaged employees were five times less likely than non-engaged employees to have a safety incident and seven times less likely to have a lost-time safety incident (Vance 2006).

Profitability

The bottom-line motivation for many organizations is to create profits to share with their stakeholders – investors, employees, and the community. In their global workforce study, Towers Watson (2012) found that companies with the lowest level of engagement had an average operating margin of 10 percent. Those with traditionally high engagement scores had a margin of 14 percent. The study found that companies with inspired employees – those who have not only the willingness but also the physical, emotional, and social energy to invest extra effort – have operating margins almost double those of companies with less-engaged employees.

When employees struggle from lack of fit they become indifferent toward their jobs – or worse, they outright loathe their work, supervisors, and organizations. They can cost their organizations money and can even destroy work units and businesses.

As one of our survey respondents said, "Work misfit, which for me is often caused by lack of challenges/interest in the job and/or micromanagement, often leads to a decline in my work productivity and possibly even quality, which leaves me feeling disappointed and unsatisfied, and doesn't help the company either."

Contrast this to a workforce filled with employees who are in jobs where they thrive and who are emotionally connected to the mission and purpose of their company. When employees are in the right environment they are passionate, creative, and entrepreneurial, and their enthusiasm fuels growth. These employees are involved in, enthusiastic about, and committed to their work and workplace, and they're driving the innovation, growth, and revenue that their companies need. These employees are the foundation for a company that consistently wins. When employees are enrolled to contribute their highest and best work, companies simply do better.

ASK YOURSELF . . .

- How would my organization benefit from a greater focus on helping employees find their fit?
- What change could my company make that would delight me?
- How would that change impact my performance?
- How might that change impact the company's business results?

PART IV

FINDING YOUR FIT

CHAPTER 12

Knowing Yourself and What You Want

Your visions will become clear only when you can look into your own heart. Who looks outside, dreams; who looks inside, awakes.

— Carl G. Jung

SOME PEOPLE JUST GET LUCKY – they find the right job for them, at the right time, and they can't imagine doing anything else. Rachel told us that she applied for a writing job right after graduating from college, got it, and after five years remains absolutely delighted with everything about the role. The people are her friends, the lifestyle supports her personal needs, she feels that she's paid fairly, and the work is drop-dead interesting.

For most people, the positive experience of loving your job frequently happens when you truly understand yourself. It's noteworthy that people experience less work misfit with age. Most of us, over time, develop a deeper understanding of ourselves, our needs, and the environment in which we thrive, which enables us to focus more intensely on how to partner well with others, be altruistic, listen, and take risks that facilitate a positive work fit.

When we feel miserable at work, it's all too easy to focus our energy on the flaws in our company or our job in a "grass is always greener on the other side" phenomenon that can result in fast, even reckless, moves from one job to another. Before you jump out of one difficult situation of misfit into another it's worth spending time getting to know yourself. There are two parts to work fit for you to explore: understanding your unique self and knowing the organization you belong to or want to join. In this way, fit is akin to a lock and a key, or a foot and a shoe – unless you know yourself, it's hard to find the place you fit best. Looking in the mirror and asking hard questions about work fit will enable you to efficiently and proactively ensure that you're taking steps that make sense and, above all else, won't land you in an even worse situation.

In 1989, Professor Ed Tomey of Antioch University New England inspired Moe with a statement she'll always remember: "There are two critical questions to being effective at work: Who am I? and Who am I with you?" Our research took us back repeatedly to the critical role of the first question – Who am I? – in discovering great work fit. Self-discovery is a lifelong process that forms in layers, over time, as we mature and grow.

We found the following personal characteristics to be particularly helpful for understanding yourself as you consider whether a job is right for you, or as you search for a new company or role. These are:

- **Your Personal Strengths and Impact on Others** – Knowing what you're really good at, understanding where you need to change, and realistically assessing the impact you have on others are key to assessing work fit.

- **Your Life Stage** – Your needs for income, adventure, stability, learning, travel, and many other variables change as you get older.

- **Your Flexibility Needs** – Understanding your ability to be flexible (travel, varied work hours) or your need for your job to be flexible (freedom to set your own work hours) will help you determine what to look for in a job or organization.

- **Your Learning and Development Needs** – The basic human need to grow and evolve varies by individual and circumstances, and knowing what you need can make a difference between a miserable stuck feeling and a delightful work fit.

- **Your Aspirations and Dreams** – Oftentimes, where you are today with your work situation is a waypoint on the path to where you dream of being. Aspirations inspire, motivate, and matter.

Personal Strengths and Impact

The ancient Greek aphorism "know thyself" has been attributed to many, and it has stood the test of time as a maxim for basic human effectiveness. In fact, understanding your own needs, desires, preferences, and opinions helps you better interact with others. When you realistically assess your inner motivations and outer impact, you foster a great capacity for positive influence in your environment and with the people around you. Daniel Goleman, researcher and writer in the realm of emotional intelligence, defines self-awareness as the first big step toward more effectively navigating relationships in the world. Self-awareness is essential in navigating your search for the right job. It's tempting to think of self-awareness primarily as noticing your weaknesses or growth needs, but it's important to also focus on understanding and appreciating your strengths and assets.

Malcolm told us that when he hit 35 he knew he needed a job change, but he really wasn't sure what kind of change was going to be best for him. Work was becoming less and less fulfilling, and he noticed that he was thinking a lot about retirement, which was still a long way off. A friend suggested that he consider an in-depth personality assessment system such as the Enneagram (see enneagraminstitute.com), and through his company he was able to gather 360-degree feedback about his leadership impact. This system provided nuanced dimensions of self-knowledge and awareness for Malcolm, helping him to identify his core personal needs, his natural leadership strengths, and the environment he would most likely thrive in.

As Malcolm discovered, there are many ways that you can deepen your self-knowledge and awareness. Doing so will facilitate a more rigorous and honest exploration of the best environment, role, and organization for you.

We each bring unique human qualities to how we approach our work. Beyond the specifics of executing tasks based on our knowledge, training, and experience, how we work includes the varied ways we might resolve an issue. Certain approaches work better in some work environments than others, and the extent to which we know our natural inclinations and habits will determine how we show up in a work situation. This aspect of self-exploration is avoided by many of us since we often don't have time at work to think about our own impact – the pace and volume of work squeeze out reflective time. Developing a practice of claiming time to think about yourself and your ideal work setting will increase your odds of finding a positive work fit.

Tools to Help You Become More Self-Aware

Get a Personality or Style Assessment

There are a number of cost-effective, reliable, and valid personality or behavioral style assessments on the market today. These are often completed online, cost from $25 to $85 per person, and only take about 30 minutes to score. Our favorites include the Everything DiSC Workplace Assessment distributed by Wiley Publishing, the Hogan (measuring "the dark side, the bright side, and the inside"), the Emotional Intelligence Appraisal distributed by Talent Smart, Strengths Finder by Gallup, and the Enneagram. Whatever assessment tool you choose, you'll want a statistically reliable assessment (your scores are consistent over time) that has high face validity (it feels accurate when you read it). Appendix 3, "Assessment Tool Comparison Chart" helps you compare the different assessment tools.

When completing a self-assessment, remember to stay focused while you score it, and think about yourself in the context of your specific situation. All of these assessments are accompanied by a thorough report with suggestions for applying the concepts in your life, and most will also suggest an expert to assist in interpreting your results. Behavioral or personality assessments describe nuanced aspects of you, and expert interpretation can help you map your unique traits to the cultural or other work qualities that are a great fit for you.

Find a Peer Coach or a Peer Group

Another cost-effective tool for self-awareness is a peer group in your profession or a friend or colleague who will serve as a peer coach as you examine your strengths, assets, and opportunities. Counsel this coach on what you're seeking to learn more about yourself, share with them any assessment information you have, and ask them to provide support in your quest to understand yourself. Some possible questions to provide them include:

- Do you think this assessment reflects how you see me? Why or why not?

- I feel that my strengths and weakness are_____. What else do you see as my strengths and weaknesses as a colleague or team member?

- What do you know about me that I may not be able to see on my own? What impact do I have on others?

- What feedback do you have for me about the kind of work environment in which I seem to do my best?

- What sometimes bugs you about how I behave, and do you think that I should work on this?

What matters the most is establishing an explicit agreement for support on a particular issue – in this case, self-awareness as a prerequisite to finding a great work fit. We suggest an explicit request with a defined duration, for example, "Jamie, I wonder if you would be willing to meet with me for two sessions in the next four weeks to help me increase my self-awareness as I contemplate my job situation."

Ask Around Often

Even if you don't ask one person to be your peer coach, another way to develop self-awareness is to ask people around you for their perspectives and opinions about you. People you trust, who have your best interests at heart, are usually the best sources for realistic and helpful feedback about the impact you have, the strengths they love, and the things they find challenging about you. Rarely do we see or experience ourselves the way others do. Much like a singer whose voice sounds different to them than it does to an audience, the best way to understand your impact is to ask others openly and honestly about it. Doing so puts you in a position of vulnerability, which researcher Brené Brown defines as "uncertainty, risk, and emotional exposure." Making yourself vulnerable calls for courage. So, take a deep breath and remember your end goal (self-awareness) and start asking people what they notice about you (really!). What you learn will be enormously useful; it's not a score of positives or negatives that you seek, but the most accurate, unbiased picture possible of the complex being that is you.

Some questions to start with are:

- What do you see as my natural gifts?

- What do you think makes me hard to work with?

- Based on what you know about my work situation right now, where do you see me thriving or struggling?

- What's your biggest wish for me for my work situation?

- I'm working on changing my behavior regarding _____. Have you noticed any improvement or change lately?

- What else do you think that I can do to be more effective in that arena?

360-Degree Feedback

Another excellent option for building self-awareness is to get 360-degree feedback via a multi-rater assessment by your boss, colleagues, direct reports, and others. This kind of assessment gives you insights into the impact you have on others in a confidential and anonymous way, and it's particularly useful for people in leadership roles. With a price ranging from $250 to $580 (in addition to the costs of expert interpretation and coaching), 360-degree feedback can be a fast, effective, and valuable reality check as to how you come across, your strengths, and the things that get in your way. We recommend using a third-party coach or consultant to administer the assessment, and our favorites include the Leadership Practices Inventory, the Hogan Lead, 360 Refined, and the Center for Creative Leadership's Benchmarks Suite.

If you have a 360-degree assessment done on yourself, remember to take notice of your strengths as well as your weaknesses. Most of us tend to focus on criticism, but being able to objectively understand what you do well can greatly increase the positive impact you have. By understanding through the lens of other people how you come across, you'll be able to make positive changes where necessary to increase your effectiveness, while you also gain insight into the type of situation in which you'll flourish. Ken, a coaching client, said it this way: "When I got the feedback from the 360 it confirmed what I already knew but hadn't been willing to admit to myself. I do best in an environment with clear processes and structure. Without these in place in my current company, I had become a bit of a micromanaging boss. This made it hard for folks who worked for me. I either needed to lead differently or find an environment in which my need for rules was more practical. A tech start-up was not that place!"

Hire a Professional

If you have personal financial resources or company support, it can help to hire a coach to assist you in gathering data and feedback that will heighten your self-awareness and self-understanding. Coaching is a one-to-one process of support and guidance that can help you make progress toward your specific goal or behavior change. We recommend a trained professional who operates from a best-practice code of ethics and who is experienced with situations such as yours. Consider asking your employer's people development or HR department for help in finding a coach, and ask colleagues whom you admire what resources they might recommend for self-development. You may want to familiarize yourself with the standards of the International Coach Federation and interview a coach to determine if they're a good match for you. Executive coaching can cost anywhere from $200 to $600 per hour, and a personal life coach can cost between $75 and $300 per hour (Rothman and WanVeer 2008). You'll get the most value out of coaching if you employ regular intervals of learning, practice, discussion, and application. Coaching often lasts several months.

ASK YOURSELF . . .

- Which of these approaches to learning more about me is appealing?

- What steps might I take to get started?

Stage of Life

Most of us seek work fit during our adult years, which is our longest period of human development. But adulthood is not one long unbroken block of unchanging needs and desires; it's filled with nuanced stages. In our research and experience we've discovered the following approximate stages of adult, work-related development:

- **Exploration** – These are our early years of professional development, when we're selecting a career while we're still in school or testing options after school. In this period flexibility is key as we try new things. We're often not financially independent and may be underpaid in our work (internships, for example).

Meaning often surfaces in this stage as a priority, as we assess what matters to us in the world and where and how we want to contribute.

- **Early Real Life** – It's in this stage that we often begin to settle into a specific career or field. We're financially independent, and we're highly flexible if we don't yet have the responsibilities of spouse, partner, or children. Our direction is unfolding, and we have likely landed in one occupation, at least for now,

- **Milestone** – In this period, we often enter parenting or partnering, and we may seek a more permanent residence or less rigorous or lengthy travel. We often seek core stability, if not permanence, and are accumulating jobs and experience that matter to our resume and reputation. Many people move from being an individual contributor at work to being a manager or leader. Flexible work hours may be important during early parenting years. And many workers are proving their competence in this stage as they develop a reputation with capstone or reward moments (advanced degrees, honorary awards, etc.).

- **Maturing** – At this stage, some people transition out of full-time work arrangements. They may become caregivers for older parents, becoming part of the sandwich generation (caring for their parents and their children at the same time). People can find new meaning at this stage as they seek to give back to the community or leave a legacy.

As we transition from one stage of life to another, our needs change, but this doesn't necessarily mean that we'll need to change jobs. Ideally, as our needs and interests change our workplace will support and enable these changes through projects, promotions, new areas of responsibility, or even job shifts. This way we'll maintain our feelings of positive fit.

ASK YOURSELF . . .

- Which life stage am I in right now?
- How might my current life stage affect my ranking of the six elements of work fit?

Your stage of life isn't dependent on your age, but rather it's determined by the types of activities and work that you're doing at the time. You can change your circumstance at any age (have a family, divorce, pursue an advanced degree, etc.), which can change your needs, interests, and inter-dependencies, and, as a result, change what you need from your work.

Our stage of life is different for each of us. Susan said, "I was a new mother and was unable to work remotely one day a week. This felt irrational to me, so I moved on." Or consider Daniel, who said, "I couldn't continue at that job, because of its intensity, while continuing my education." And Marilyn spoke about the interdependency of stage of life and work fit: "I felt I outgrew my last role. I had a great relationship with my boss and team, a lot of leadership and visibility, but there was no more room for growth, which mattered more to me as I matured." Carefully consider what matters to you at your particular stage of life so that you know, realistically, what kind of job or company will feel best for you at that time.

Most of us will have many jobs over the course of our lives, so it's helpful to adopt an "it all made sense at the time" attitude when you pick a job based on your stage of life. What make sense when you're young, single, and motivated to travel and learn may not make sense at all when you're mid-career, carrying high financial obligations, and eager to ensure a safe retirement. Long gone are the days of having one career, much less one job lasting for our entire adult life. Loyalty alone is no longer keeping workers in place in organizations; instead, stage of life, work-life balance, personal ambition, and an interest in learning have become the components of thriving in a job.

The skill of being able to notice, describe, and proclaim what matters to you at a particular stage of life will help you to determine whether a role is a good fit for you. Doing so may mean that you change jobs more often than your parents did, or, in some cases, you may stay put. The important thing is to consider whether your job is meeting your needs at your stage of life, rather than assume that one job will satisfy your changing needs.

Flexibility Needs

In our high-tech, global, services-based economy, control over your work schedule is a key determinant of work fit. Flexibility includes the ability to control your work arrival and departure times, the chance to take midday time for personal or caregiving needs, work-at-home options, and other strategies that enable you to do the things that you need and want to do. Understand your habits, responsibilities, commute requirements, and productivity traits so that you can assess what type of flexibility at work matters to you.

Recent research, such as an Ernst and Young study of 9,700 employees in the world's largest economies, suggests that flexibility is an increasingly important currency for workers (Sahadi 2015). And in their article "A Revolutionary Change: Making the Workplace More Flexible," authors Jolynn Shoemaker, Amy Brown, and Rachel Barbour (2011) suggest that "We need leaders who understand that adaptability is necessary in a rapidly changing world and that workplace flexibility is a key component of keeping pace with change." One of the assumptions of the accountability model developed by Brown and Barbour is "That all workers will need to adjust the time they spend doing paid and unpaid work at various stages of their lives." They also emphasize that it's important that companies change policies and practices over time that leverage the benefits of enhanced workplace flexibility. Flexibility is increasingly important.

For some workers, flexibility includes the ability to work at home on some days. For others flexibility takes the form of being able to modify their schedule based on caregiving, educational, recreational, or other needs, in particular being able to change arrival and departure times.

At the center of the flexibility dimension of work fit is the desire of people to manage the expectations of their jobs along with their caregiving duties. While caregiving has historically been primarily the responsibility of women, more and more men are now seeking creative workplace options that allow them to manage the entirety of their lives, including caregiving, rather than sacrificing their family and personal obligations to work long, untenable hours. Anne Marie Slaughter has written extensively on the changing cultural and structural patterns that continue to face working parents, especially women. Slaughter (2015) writes, "Real flexibility – the kind that gives you at least some measure of control over when and how you work in a week, a month, a year and over the course of a career – is a critical part of the solution of how to fit work and care together."

To assess your need for flexibility ask yourself these questions:

ASK YOURSELF . . .

- Can I work regular daytime hours every day?
- What schedule works best for me and my productivity habits?
- Do I have outside interests or caregiving demands that would be well served by a particular type of flexibility?
- How do I feel about commute time?
- Do I prefer working at home?

Learning Needs and Opportunity to Progress

What Abraham Maslow first defined as self-actualization needs (realizing personal potential, self-fulfillment, peak experiences, and personal growth) remain critical aspects of successful work fit. Most of us seek to progress throughout our lives rather than stagnate. According to our research, people who left a job most often cited a lack of opportunity to grow as their reason for job unhappiness. And people who were happy at their jobs rated their opportunity to learn and grow as a top reason for their contentment. Mary said it this way, "My exit was less about a poor fit than it was that I grew out of the place. After 12 years, I just didn't think I was learning, and, in fact, neither was the company. That's just bad all around."

If you're feeling stagnant in your role you're not alone. Training programs and opportunities to grow are frequently rated as critical elements for finding a good fit at work (Deloitte 2016), but we're not always able to focus on learning because of other priorities and pressures. There are times when we're busily tending to other dimensions of our lives, and simply doing our jobs and going home at night is all we can handle. So how can you think of learning at work?

Aspirations and Dreams

As we interviewed people about work fit, we were amazed to find that many landed in their most successful roles through a series of accidents. In fact, the simple act of moving on from a misstep is an essential element of resilience and growth. One person described it as "several key game-show-like decisions: what's behind door number 1, 2, or 3. I randomly chose, and over the years the resultant path has made total sense."

We often choose jobs based on our current circumstances, stage of life, job availability, and other interdependent variables, hoping that the direction we're moving will turn out well. In many cases, because of the trade-offs we make for work fit, we find ourselves in a job that's clearly just a waypoint on a road taking us somewhere else. Pete was a maritime engineer who worked at an engineering firm in Philadelphia right out of college. His dream was to work as a chief mate or second mate on a tanker, but he felt that he should cut his teeth by working in an engineering house shoreside to show his ability to work analytically and to build his resume. Or consider Wendy, who took a job as a programmer early in her career even though her hope was to be an analyst working with big data. To be seen at a future date as a candidate for big data jobs, Wendy needed to prove herself on the programming battlefield first.

Each job decision we make matters, but they're not usually catastrophic. In fact, our research tells us that it's the jobs people picked that are a poor fit that often result in them finding a great fit. The contrast helps us discover what's best for us, and it also helps us clarify our hopes, dreams, and fantasies. Many of us fail to allow ourselves to imagine our wildest dreams, but allowing ourselves to think big and dream can often create the motivation and the space to get closer to them than we imagined possible. If you haven't done so already, consider the long-term view – where you're heading and what your life's goals are – and spend some time crystalizing your thinking by asking questions like these:

ASK YOURSELF . . .

- Where do I see myself when I think ahead to my dream job in ten years?

- Are there credentials or experiences that I lack that are required for that job?

- What lifestyle and financial dimensions will matter to me in ten years?

- Are there dreams that my partner, friends, family, and I share that could impact the work I pursue?

- What risks am I willing to take to achieve this dream?

A great work fit means that you're learning and growing. Every job has boring aspects on any given day, but what matters for great work fit is an overall feeling that you're increasing your capacity, and thereby fulfilling a basic human need.

Consider doing the exercise in Figure 12-1 as you imagine your ideal work fit.

Notice which parts of your ideal day matter deeply to you. These items are likely representative of some of your deeply held values and act as guiding lights to what you hold dear. If you land at a company that doesn't consider a value of yours important, or at least relevant, you'll likely feel misfit. While personal values are different from organizational values and serve a different purpose, the clearer you can be about the dimensions of work that you value highly, the more likely you'll be able to evaluate a potential company with open eyes.

What Gets in the Way of Self-Awareness?

It's a rigorous journey, this voyage toward self-awareness. It requires honesty, energy, openness, and humility. Watch out for barriers to increasing your self-awareness – these barriers can impact your ability to find the

Ideal Day Exercise

Take a minute and recall a day in your work life in which you felt that everything just clicked. As you reflect on your ideal day at work, consider which aspects might contribute to the right work fit for you. Those aspects likely reflect things that matter to you. Write them down.

- What were you doing?
- Were you in your office or cubicle or on the road?
- Were you at a client or customer location?
- Why did you feel energized?
- With whom were you interacting during this positive experience?
- What were you learning?
- What time of day was it?
- Did you feel comfortable and good about the effort required?
- What was the task like: ambiguous and complex or clear and specific (or something in the middle)?
- What goals were you striving toward, and where had you learned them?
- How were you dressed?

Figure 12-1. This exercise will help you image what your ideal work fit looks like.

work situation that's ideal for you at this time in your life. The primary things that people told us got in the way are:

- **Ego and Lack of Humility** – It's easy to mistake confidence (ego) for arrogance, which is the feeling that you're better or smarter than other people. Don't limit your sense of yourself to your own view; combining your view with those of the people around you will give you a more rounded and realistic vision of yourself.

- **Self-Protection/Shame Triggers** – When you begin to look within and examine your needs, motivations, and strengths, you may see things that you don't like. This can interfere with your sense of work fit, and it can prompt a cascade of negative feelings if you're driven to prove your competence or defend yourself. Listen to the voice in your head that tells you about you. Manage negative thoughts by showering yourself with self-compassion. As Kristen Neff (2015) says, "This is a moment of suffering. Suffering is part of life. May I be kind to myself in this moment. May I give myself the compassion I need."

- **Perceptions of Others** – We've heard story after story of people who ignore their own needs and preferences because of the pressure they feel from those around them. Resist feeling that you're obligated to, or should, define success by what others think. By carefully understanding your needs, dreams, desires, and ideal work environment, you'll come to understand what you truly need to thrive. Examine your own assumptions and judgments first, and stay true to what you want.

- **Confirmation Bias** – Just because you really want a job to be a great fit for you doesn't mean that it is. You must guard against your own confirmation bias when you're considering work fit (Heshmat 2015). When you deeply want something to be true, you often end up believing that it is true, and thus you stop paying attention to evidence to the contrary.

- **Lack of Time to Think** – One of the most frequent complaints Moe hears in her consulting practice, from leaders at all levels, is that they simply don't get enough time to think. To truly examine the complex nature of your work fit, you need some time to ask the right questions and look honestly at the situation you face. Oftentimes when people are feeling the budding realities of misfit, they try to solve the problem by getting even busier than normal rather than by slowing down to consider what's happening. There are ways to remedy poor work fit, and they don't all involve leaving your job.

ASK YOURSELF . . .

- What do I need to do to create more time for myself to simply think about and process what's going on?

Self-awareness is a lifelong process. Comfortably settling into a job for a lifetime is a reality no more. Thus, developing the lifelong practice of being self-aware facilitates your ability to be resilient, realistic, and responsive, modifying your work fit when it begins to feel less than ideal. If your work fit is poor, the person with the most ability to influence, modify, and change the situation is YOU. Look within, ask the hard questions, and pay attention to your feelings, thoughts, needs, and desires. Self-awareness, above all else, is the starting point to making work fit better.

CHAPTER 13

Calculating the Elements and Weighing Trade-Offs

When someone makes a decision, he is really diving into a strong current that will carry him places he had never dreamed of when he first made the decision.

— Paul Coelho, *The Alchemist*

W E EACH HAVE A DIFFERENT WORK FIT CALCULATION. In fact, we have many different calculations over the course of our lives. What you want is to know *your* calculation at this moment in time. But before we go any further, here's a warning:

PERFECT WORK FIT DOES NOT EXIST

While we believe that fit really matters to you and the world, our research and experience tells us that work fit is always a series of trade-offs that are related to many factors, including the six elements of fit and your stage of life, even when you're really, really thriving and content at work. What makes sense today simply may not make sense tomorrow, and this fact means that you'll be calculating how you fit in your work situation many, many times in the course of your life.

Getting Started

Your work fit calculation requires reflection and analysis of each of the six elements of work fit (meaning, job, culture, relationship, lifestyle, and financial), individually as well as in total. Our research shows that people who are really happy at work, love their jobs, and feel a high degree of work fit have at least three of the core elements working for them, and none of the elements is causing regular pain.

We suggest that you start with your answers to the checklists for each element that you reviewed in earlier chapters in order to get a full picture of your current work fit. We've combined those checklists in Figure 13-1 to make it easier to review all your answers in one place.

THE SIX ELEMENTS CHECKLIST
MEANING FIT   Meaning fit exists when you feel that what you do matters.
☐ The things I care about also seem to matter to my company.
☐ I regularly feel sure that I'm contributing to something important.
☐ I am clear about what I contribute.
☐ I am satisfied that what I do makes a difference most of the time.
☐ My job taps into my interests and passions.
☐ I feel pride in working for this company.
▇ How many items did you check for meaning fit? _____

Checklist 13-1. For each element of fit, check the statements that apply to you. Start with your assessments for each element that you made in earlier chapters in order to get a full picture of your current work fit. We've combined those checklists here to make it easier to review all your answers in one place. Total the number of checks for each element and enter that number in the space provided.

JOB FIT
Job fit exists when the responsibilities of the job align with your talents.

☐ My job is a good match for my skills, interests, training, and talents.

☐ I have opportunities at work to do what I really enjoy.

☐ My job makes good use of my previous experience.

☐ I have the right resources and support to perform my job.

☐ I feel that I am learning and growing in my job.

☐ I have the credentials and education needed to do my job well.

How many items did you check for job fit? _____

CULTURE FIT
Culture fit exists when your values and beliefs are compatible with the practices of your employer.

☐ The organization's actions match its values.

☐ My communication style works well here.

☐ I feel fully engaged.

☐ I understand my role and my job.

☐ I am able to be myself.

☐ Processes are consistent and reliable.

How many items did you check for culture fit? _____

Checklist 13-1 continued.

RELATIONSHIP FIT

Relationship fit exists when you like and respect the people you work with and you receive appropriate support and trust to do your job.

☐ My boss and I share similar work-related values and philosophies.

☐ I generally trust my boss and we communicate well with each other.

☐ I enjoy spending time with my coworkers.

☐ I feel respected and trust my coworkers.

☐ I have good friends at work.

☐ Conflict is healthy and productive here.

▉ **How many items did you check for relationship fit?** _____

LIFESTYLE FIT

Lifestyle fit exists when your life outside of work is supported by your employer's policies and practices.

☐ I feel that I have the right balance between my job and time outside of work.

☐ I find my work challenging but not overwhelming.

☐ There isn't pressure to work long hours that interferes with my life outside of work.

☐ I feel that I can meet my personal and family needs while also working productively.

☐ My job is flexible in the ways I need it to be.

☐ Travel to and from work is convenient.

▉ **How many items did you check for lifestyle fit?** _____

Checklist 13-1 continued.

FINANCIAL FIT

Financial fit exists when you feel that you are paid fairly and when your overall compensation meets your needs.

☐ I feel that my pay is fair.

☐ I appreciate my overall compensation package, long- and short-term.

☐ There's a good match between my job and my pay.

☐ There's a good match between my job and my benefits.

☐ I can take care of my responsibilities with what I'm paid.

☐ There's room for growth in my pay over time.

▉ **How many items did you check for financial fit?** _____

Checklist 13-1 continued.

Congratulations! You now have a reasonably good assessment of how you're feeling at the moment about your current work situation.

ASK YOURSELF . . .

- Which elements had the most items checked? The least?
- Does this surprise me?
- Do my scores surprise me? Why or why not?
- Have the highest-scoring elements been areas of satisfaction at my job for a long time?
- Are there at least three elements that have more than four items checked?
- How low are the lowest scores?

What your scores might indicate:

- If you have at least one area that has zero or one items checked, your work fit may be causing you serious pain.

- If you have at least three elements with more than four items checked, there's a lot that's working for you in your current situation. Congratulations on a solid fit!

- If you have no areas with zero or one items checked, you're probably not experiencing pain in any element. Congratulations – you're not suffering too much.

It's always possible, however, that no matter what your score you may be feeling unhappy at work. This has to do with what in particular matters to you right now. (And be sure to resist comparing your feelings to what others are feeling – they may or may not have the same needs, interests, or priorities that you do.)

Understanding What Matters to You Right Now

No matter how you assessed your current situation, you need to understand what really matters to you right now to begin the process of improving your work fit. Perhaps you now have to deal with your aging parent, so a flexible schedule has become a priority. Or maybe your spouse recently took a job in another city and you're worried about commute times. Or maybe you've started worrying about having enough money for retirement and are now working hard to save money, making financial fit a top priority. Take a few minutes and consider your stage of life, what you know about yourself, and your aspirations, and score each work fit element on how much it matters to you now (1 = not a very important element to you right now; 5 = a very important element to you right now). Use Table 13-1 to record your answers.

WHAT MATTERS TO YOU?	
Fit Element	Importance
Meaning	
Job	
Culture	
Relationship	
Lifestyle	
Financial	

Figure 13-1. Rate the importance of each element of fit on a scale of 1 to 5 with 1=low importance and 5=high importance.

ELEMENTS OF FIT TO FOCUS ON IMPROVING			
Fit Element	What Matters Most to You?	How Does Your Current Job Rate?	Differential
Meaning			
Job			
Culture			
Relationship			
Lifestyle			
Financial			

Figure 13-2. Enter your scores from Figure 13-1 in the what matters most to you column. Then enter scores on how your current job rates on the same scale from 1=low to 5=high. In the differential column subtract your current job rating from what matters most to you. Those elements of fit that matter most to you but have a large differential are those that you want to consider improving.

Now let's put all your scores together. Look at what matters to you and what your current situation provides to identify any major disconnects. Use Table 13-2 to highlight the areas of focus you want to consider. Let's look at an example (see Figure 13-3).

PETER EXAMPLE: ELEMENTS OF FIT HE SHOULD FOCUS ON			
Fit Element	What Matters Most to You?	How Does Your Current Job Rate?	Differential
Meaning	2	4	-2
Job	5	2	3
Culture	2	2	0
Relationship	4	2	2
Lifestyle	1	5	-4
Financial	4	3	1

Figure 13-3. In this example it's fairly clear that Peter should focus first on improving his job fit (finding a new job either within his organization or with a new organization).

Peter is an ambitious, mid-career marketing executive who wants to move into a CMO role soon. He's willing to work long hours, relocate his family, and take a salary cut for the opportunity to elevate his strategic responsibilities and prove he can handle a broader role. The job he currently has is for a company whose mission inspires him, and it afforded him the flexibility he needed while his children were young, but now he seeks a mentor and a more challenging role. It's time for a change, but he feels that he can take his time to find the right match. Peter says, "I'm grateful for my current job, but I feel ready for a bigger challenge. I believe I can do a CMO role, and I feel highly motivated." What Peter seeks next is greater job fit, an improved mentor relationship, and more financial incentives. It's not urgent that he change jobs, but he's clear about what he wants to seek next.

As you compare the elements that matter the most to you right now with the elements in your current job, what do you notice? Pay particular attention to how many items you're well-satisfied with in your current role and how these compare to what matters the most to you right now. In our experience, people who are very satisfied with their work fit report that at least three of the six elements are working well for them, and none of them are causing them pain. If one (or more) of the elements is rated very low in your current situation and it's something that matters a great deal to you right now, then your job is probably a poor work fit. Richard described his work fit this way: "My work life put too much stress on my personal life outside of work." And Mary said, "I started to disengage at work because of a lack of impact and support. Too often there are personal and business relationships that affect the success of a couple people within an organization, so you wonder why you're working so hard, putting in the hours, missing out on family life, with little to no progression or recognition."

Our research revealed that if one element is untenable, or too few elements are going well, the acknowledgment of poor work fit can either come slowly or with a sudden flash of awareness. Either way, when the realization hits, and you find yourself accepting that something about your work situation needs to change, it's both terrifying and liberating. As Hank said, "During the time I needed to work at a place that was a wrong fit the stress had a high toll on my health and my family life. Feeling unhappy and uncomfortable at work, I was constantly trying to change myself to fit in while also feeling hopeless that it could ever get better. It was physically and emotionally exhausting. By comparison, leaving was easy."

It can be heartbreaking, after you've looked long and hard for a great job, to discover misfit. And for many people, the fear of admitting that it isn't working keeps them stuck. Shireen said, "I was miserable because my work hours kept me away from my family, but I was scared to leave because I feared I'd be trading my seniority at that job for another equally bad job."

Doing the math and feeling misfit is a process. For some people, the decision to leave precedes their actual move by months or even years, while others can act swiftly. Whatever process unfolds for you has to make sense in the context of your life. When you admit to poor work fit, you still have to weigh the costs of leaving versus the costs of staying in order to decide to change. And for some people, just the realization of misfit is the information they need to work within their existing company to find a better fit (see Chapter 15, "Flexing to Fit").

Fit for Now

Whatever your work fit calculation revealed to you, keep in mind the phrase "fit for now." Work fit involves a series of trade-offs. Are you willing to live with the fit with element A because this job offers you a better fit with element B? In our research, we heard story after story of people who stayed in poor fit situations because one or more elements were invaluable to them at the time.

Consider Maryellen, who discovered that her job was only a good fit on one element: the job itself. As a trial attorney, Maryellen knew she needed to work in actual trials. She had a terrible lifestyle fit in her job, which provided very little time for personal growth, paid poorly, and offered her no sense of purpose. In addition, she felt very little connection to her fellow employees or her boss, whom she described as a "tyrant." Nonetheless, it was a prestigious firm, and she had a high volume of cases every day. She knew that the experience the job gave her could not be found easily elsewhere, so she stuck it out for two years until she felt that she had amassed enough solid experience as a trial attorney to move to an organization that fed her on the other fit elements.

Or consider Joe, who felt misfit on every element except financial fit. His wife was on disability because of a chronic pain condition, they had two small children, and his job paid far more than most other jobs in their town. Living close to family was critical for Joe and his wife because family members provided emotional support and care, so Joe was willing to stay at that job, for the time being, for the sake of the money.

What we heard consistently from people like Maryellen and Joe was that they clearly knew the trade-offs they were making, which went a long way toward soothing the pain and unhappiness they felt in their misfit situations. Some common trade-offs that people make include:

- Work and life balance trade-off for compensation
- Meaning and purpose trade-off for key experience
- Positive relationships trade-off for essential skill learning
- Career advancement trade-off for caregiving duties
- Culture that fits for great relationships

ASK YOURSELF . . .

- Do I feel fit or misfit in my current role?
- If fit, how will I keep this situation going well?
- If misfit, do I think a change is necessary? And in what time frame do I think I need a change?
- Is the change I envision a modification within my current organization, or do I think that I'll need to leave?
- What trade-offs am I making for this role, and how are they working for me?

As you assess your situation, remember that if your work fit is okay but not great, it may still be sufficient, or even appropriate, for you right now. Poor work fit in one element may be worth the sacrifice if great work fit in another element compensates for it.

PART V
DEALING WITH MISFIT

CHAPTER 14

Regaining Your Confidence

Don't let the noise of others' opinions drown out your own inner voice.

— Steve Jobs

WHEN WORK DOESN'T WORK IT HURTS, and it often triggers self-criticism and a loss of confidence. As you try harder and harder to fit in, you may become more and more frustrated and anxious. We've seen scores of talented, successful people, with great track records of accomplishment, become incapacitated with self-doubt as they wonder why they just can't seem to make the impact they were hoping for.

Recognizing the situation and then recovering from work misfit requires that you reconnect to a sense of your unique and amazing talents. Instead of mercilessly judging and criticizing yourself for various inadequacies or shortcomings, you need to regain a sense of your innate worth. In her ground-breaking book, *Self-Compassion,* Kristen Neff (2015) talks about the need to honor and accept our humanness. She notes that things will not always go the way you want them to. You'll encounter frustrations, experience losses, make mistakes, bump up against your limitations, and fall short of your ideals. This is the human condition, a reality shared by all of us. The more you open your heart to this reality, instead of constantly fighting against it, the more you'll be able to experience your misfit as a step in your journey rather than as a damning statement about who you are.

Brené Brown's groundbreaking research on wholeheartedness has revealed that people who possess great resilience don't fail less often or less spectacularly than others; rather, they proceed with courage even when self-doubt, fear, and failure threaten to stop them in their tracks. In her latest book, *Rising Strong,* Brown (2015) details ways in which people rise from low confidence and poor performance through vulnerability and perseverance. She uncovers the mechanics of vulnerability and why emotional curiosity – getting curious about your feelings and how they connect with the way you think and behave – is the key to rising strong when we struggle, suffer, or fail. One of our favorite expressions of hers is "the story in my own head," which is a way of describing the stories we make up about ourselves and the choices we have. Unfortunately, these stories may encourage self-doubt. What story do you tell yourself about the situation you're in? Is it based in reality, or is it formed by your own guilt, fear, anxiety, or grief? What new story can you tell yourself in order to face your situation realistically and bravely?

Frequently we're harsher and less forgiving in evaluating our own situations than we would be with a friend or family member. To create a new story, it can be useful to think about what you might do if someone else were in your situation. What advice would you give? How would you help them? Exercising self-compassion and creating a new story can start with stepping back and looking at your situation from a different perspective.

ASK YOURSELF . . .

- How has my poor work fit situation shaken my confidence?
- What's the story in my head?
- What advice would I give a friend in my situation?

Key Actions to Start Moving Forward

We've learned several techniques that you can use to make sense out of misfit and move forward to create a new story and overcome your self-doubt.

Celebrate Accomplishments

Reminding yourself of all the things that you've accomplished in the past and are accomplishing now can positively affect your attitude. In addition to keeping a to-do list, take a moment at the end of the day to make a brief have-done list. These accomplishments can be as major as closing a sale or as simple as engaging in a positive interaction with a coworker. Crafting a list like this can give you a renewed appreciation for the things you've been able to achieve for the day, which in turn can produce a little emotional boost. And keeping an ongoing list of accomplishments is useful for two scenarios: negotiating with your boss about changes in your work, or updating your resume and talking to potential employers about your accomplishments.

Try a Growth Mindset

In her book, *Mindset: The New Psychology of Success,* Stanford psychologist Carol Dweck (2007) discusses the power of our beliefs, both conscious and unconscious, and how changing them can profoundly determine our future course. Dweck describes a "fixed mindset" as the belief that our character, intelligence, and creative ability are static and unchangeable and, therefore, that success is achieved by meeting a fixed standard without failure. On the other hand, someone with a "growth mindset" thrives on a challenge and sees failure as a fertile ground for growth and change.

Taking time to think deeply about the challenges you're facing in your current role and to craft ideas for small and large changes within your control can vastly improve your mindset and your ability to see potential in a difficult situation. It also can help you to feel confident in your ability to be successful despite the difficulties. In the context of a growth mindset, the setbacks you're facing in work fit can serve as motivators and as the impetus to make changes that will help.

Turn to Trusted Partners

During times of self-doubt, you'll find it helpful to surround yourself with people who understand you, who see your strengths and weaknesses and love and accept you anyway. These supporters are safe havens with whom you can share your feelings of self-doubt because they'll listen, empathize, and remind you of your innate strengths, serving as your personal cheering squad. They have seen you at your best and can remind you of what that looks like. They may be a partner, a friend, or a former coworker. Ask for what you need from these people – sometimes it will be their advice and counsel, but other times it's just for them to be present and listen. You may also want to engage a professional life coach or counselor. These people are trained to help you objectively understand difficult situations and the feelings they trigger, and they can help you to chart a positive course forward.

Sarah experienced the pain of losing her self-confidence in a poor work fit situation, and then she regained control through honest reflection and the help of friends. After graduating with her MBA, Sarah was excited about joining a well-regarded company known for its expertise in mergers and acquisitions. The president was an alumnus of her school, and she had had great conversations with him and with the CEO. They were smart and engaging, and she felt that she could add value to the company and learn a lot. She had a brief interview with the woman who would be her direct supervisor. While the woman struck Sarah as a bit immature and overly critical of her analytic background, Sarah convinced herself that it was still a great opportunity. "By the second week I was concerned that I had made a mistake. My boss was only a few years older than me and was always trying to one-up me; like bragging about how much better her business school was than mine. She seemed to go out of her way to assert her authority. For example, she would upgrade herself when we traveled and not even wait until I got off the plane to say goodbye. She called and emailed at all hours and throughout the weekend and made me travel and work in difficult situations without offering any support."

Despite her discomfort, Sarah continued to work long hours and take on additional projects in the hopes of being able to turn the situation around. "I had always been successful. I didn't want to face the thought that I couldn't make this work. I just kept trying to work harder." After seven months of feeling used and disrespected, it came to a head when the boss ignored a long-standing request Sarah had made to not work on the evening of her birthday and sent her out of town at the last minute. "Despite my anger, I felt that I had to comply. It was only through the encouragement of friends, who pointed out the abusive treatment, that I finally got the courage to resign. It wasn't just that I was treated so poorly, it was my disappointment that the company would allow that kind of behavior. I'm so glad that I had good people in my life who could help me read the situation and who told me that it was something I shouldn't accept."

ASK YOURSELF . . .

- What have I achieved today, this week, this month that I feel good about?
- What learning might be available to me now?
- Who can I turn to for support and perspective?

Practicing Self-Care

Being unhappy or feeling frustrated at work takes a huge emotional toll. It drains energy and causes you to lose perspective. Whether you've decided to try to make your current job fit better or that it's time to leave, one of the most important things is to make sure that you're taking care of yourself. So before tackling the work situation itself, make sure that you're equipped to do your best work. When we're struggling with fit, we're battling challenges to our confidence, to our energy, to our self-esteem. Our unhappiness at work tends to push us even harder into unproductive behaviors, or it causes us to disengage. We allow the unhappiness to spill into other parts of our life. We often enter into a vicious spiral where our actions make things worse rather than better.

This is a time to honor the things in your life that give you joy and energy. You need to take extra care with your health and with the relationships that matter the most to you. Here are some relatively easy things that you can do that can make a big difference. You don't have to do everything; just pick two or three that speak to you and invest in them.

Get a Good Nights' Sleep
Sleeping poorly ruins your day. The more tired you are, the harder it is to concentrate and the more susceptible you are to feeling depressed and irritable. In turn this can create a vicious spiral – it's tough to perform

at work and you become more easily discouraged by challenges and less confident in your results.

When researchers at Harvard Medical School had adults do a task once, get a good night's sleep, and then try the task again, they showed improvement. But participants who stayed awake 30 hours after learning the same task had a much harder time improving their skills – even if they practiced and had a chance to catch some recovery shut eye later (Stickgold, James, and Hobson 2000). The initial sleep deprivation impaired their ability to learn.

Additional research shows that sleep loss has an even stronger effect on mood than it does on cognitive ability or motor function. People who sleep less tend to have more symptoms of depression, lower self-esteem, and more anxiety (Colton and Altevogt 2006).

Jeff Bezos is one of the many executives who talk about the benefits of sleep. In various interviews he has shared that eight hours of sleep gives him the alertness and clarity of thought necessary to tackle each day's challenges. Even in the difficult early years of Amazon, instead of sacrificing rest to work around the clock building his company, Bezos ended his day and went to bed.

There are numerous guides to getting a good night's sleep with techniques that include discovering your optimal sleep schedule, boosting your melatonin, or making your bedroom more sleep-friendly. Read up on the methods available and experiment to find what works best for you. When you're struggling at work you need all the strength you can muster, and getting a good night's sleep is more critical than ever.

Take a Break

It's becoming more common to go through our workdays without stopping. We take pride in a calendar that's filled with appointments from start to finish. We eat lunch at our desk while catching up on emails. We even know executives who schedule individual meetings with direct reports while walking from one conference room to another! Being busy has become a badge of honor.

A growing body of evidence, however, including a study from the University of Illinois at Urbana-Champaign, shows that taking regular breaks from mental tasks improves productivity and creativity – and that skipping breaks can lead to stress and exhaustion (Ariga and Lleras

2011). Even something as simple as looking away from your keyboard for at least five minutes every hour to rest your mind and eyes can make a difference.

Scheduling downtime at work isn't selfish, it's not a sign of weakness, it's not a signal of inefficiency – it's a crucial part of doing your best work. If you work long hours alone on a computer, set an alarm to remind yourself to get up and stretch every hour. Set up lunch with a colleague or a friend. Get outside for a quick walk in the afternoon.

If you have a job that's filled with meetings, mark out time every day on your calendar for reflection. Jeff Weiner, the famously hard-charging CEO of LinkedIn, purposely schedules 30- to 90-minute blocks of "nothing" in his calendar for personal time and reflection. He says that while these periods of nothing first felt like indulgences, he realized over time that "not only were these breaks important, they were absolutely necessary in order for me to do my job." He suggests that you "think big, catch up on the latest industry news, get out from under that pile of unread emails, or just take a walk."

When you're struggling with fit, one of the most important things is not to just react to events and emotions but to take time to step back and reflect on your experiences. Taking a daily break, or, better yet, a long weekend or vacation, is a great start.

Get Some Exercise

We're all well aware of the benefits of regular exercise for physical health and stamina. What's equally important is the benefit for our mood. Physical activity stimulates various brain chemicals that may leave you feeling happier and more relaxed. Exercise and physical activity deliver oxygen and nutrients to your tissues, which in turn gives you more energy.

Exercise doesn't have to be a huge time commitment. According to a recent study in the Journal of the American College of Cardiology, running just five minutes a day can provide the same health benefits as running much more (Lee et al. 2014). Exercise could be as simple as walking up the stairs at work or as ambitious as participating in your first triathlon, but engage in some type of physical activity – it will improve your mood and confidence, and it will equip you to think more clearly about your situation at work.

Write in a Journal

Keeping a journal is useful not just for writers and teenage girls. Meebo co-founder Elaine Wherry kept a *100 Mistakes Diary*, which she credits for helping to guide her team through its 2012 acquisition by Google. Black Eyed Peas front woman Fergie used her journal to help kick an addiction to crystal meth and to set goals to write a number one song and win a Grammy. Filmmaker George Lucas takes a pocket notebook everywhere for writing down ideas, inspirations, and possible plot angles.

It works for work, too: a Harvard Business School study found that people who wrote about their jobs improved their performance by 23 percent (Stefano et al. 2016). The process of reflecting will boost your learning and increase your confidence and ultimately your performance.

You can journal with a digital tool such as Evernote or in a personal blog on WordPress.com. You can write with a fine pen in a beautiful handcrafted notebook. You can doodle with colored pencils. You can snap photos of things that represent your day. You can adhere to a strict regimen, like writing three pages a day, as suggested by Julia Cameron (2002) in *The Artist's Way*, or you can simply take five minutes to jot down accomplishments, inspirations, and observations. You can rant about your boss or dream about your future. You don't write for anyone to read; you write simply for you to record. The important thing is tapping into the power that comes from documenting your thoughts – this both diffuses their ability to distract you and unleashes their ability to inform you. Figure 14-1 offers some prompts to help you with daily journaling.

Try a Digital Detox

Technology has taken over our lives and enabled the workday to stretch far beyond its traditional boundaries. According to a study by retailer Pixmania, smartphones have people in Britain working an extra two hours a day (Pan 2012). Our experience working and traveling around the world suggests that this isn't unique.

For some people, on some occasions, the expanded use of technology can be a good thing. Technology can enable you to leave the office early to catch a child's soccer game while still keeping an eye on a critical work situation. It may make it possible to relax more on a vacation if you know that you won't have to triage hundreds of emails on the day you return. But is it really making us more productive to answer emails

Daily Journal Questions

- What did I enjoy today?
- Who did I enjoy being with?
- What did I do really well today?
- What inspired me?
- What did I improve or improve upon?
- What did I learn?
- How can I do things better tomorrow?
- Where did I get energy?
- What was frustrating to deal with today?

Figure 14-1. Questions you might consider asking yourself for your daily journal.

throughout the evening, on the weekends, and on our holidays? Are we really better because we're always on?

John Pencavel (2014) of Stanford University studied the relationship between working hours and productivity among British munitions workers. What he found was that there was a non-linear relationship between working hours and output. Below 49 weekly hours, variations in output are proportional to variations in hours. But when people worked more than about 50 hours, output rose at a decreasing rate. Output at 70 hours of work differed little from output at 56 hours. That extra 14 hours of work was a waste of time.

While it might be challenging to cut your actual hours at work, you may be able to limit how you allow technology to expand them. Some studies have found that excessive reliance on technology can make us more distracted, impatient, and forgetful (Parker-Pope 2010). More and more individuals are electing to take weekly "technology shabbats," and many of us are looking for ways to live our tech-saturated lives more mindfully (Headspace 2013, Shlain 2012). This practice can be particularly useful when you need to gain a fresh perspective on the difference in fit between your current work and your desired work.

David Mintz, CEO and founder of Tofutti Brands, picks one night a week to turn his smartphone off completely. He uses that night to clear his head and remove himself from his work life. "Taking a break is a good thing for you – smartphones can cloud judgment," he says. "Clearing your life every once in a while of distractions will make you a better business owner or employee and improve your career."

Take Some Deep Breaths

The term "fight or flight" is also known as the stress response. It's what the body does as it prepares to confront or avoid danger. The cause doesn't have to be life threatening. Challenges such as difficult coworkers, lack of resources, or intense pressure to perform can create stress. In turn the stress response can suppress the immune system, increasing susceptibility to illnesses, and it can contribute to anxiety and depression.

A counter to the stress response is to invoke the relaxation response, which is accomplished by using a breathing technique first developed in the 1970s at Harvard Medical School by cardiologist Dr. Herbert Benson (Benson and Klipper 2000). The key to relaxed breathing is to engage the diaphragm, bringing the air in through your nose, completely filling your lungs, and allowing your lower belly to rise; then exhale slowly through your mouth. Deep breathing can be a beneficial daily practice, and, at a minimum, it's a good way to step back and ground yourself when the workday becomes particularly challenging.

Practice Mindfulness

Though it has its roots in Buddhist meditation, the secular practice of mindfulness has entered the American mainstream in recent years, with thousands of studies documenting its physical and mental health benefits. Companies such as Google, Facebook, and Twitter have added mindfulness classes, rooms for quiet meditation, and even practices such as "mindful lunches," conducted in complete silence except for the ringing of prayer bells.

Mindfulness involves acceptance, meaning that you pay attention to thoughts and feelings without judging them – without believing, for instance, that there's a right or wrong way to think or feel at a given moment. When you practice mindfulness, your thoughts tune in to what you're sensing at the present moment, rather than rehashing the past or imagining the future. There are lots of online resources and even great mobile apps to help you get started with a mindfulness practice. Below we've outlined a simple approach:

- Choose a time when you have ten minutes to yourself, and find a quiet place to sit comfortably.

- Acknowledge any thoughts or judgments you have about starting your mindfulness practice. Our minds are constantly thinking, so you may want to notice whether you're caught up in thoughts as you get ready for your practice. If that's the case, simply acknowledge the thoughts and emotions that come into your awareness, and then refocus on getting settled and comfortable.

- Once you're settled and comfortable, you can choose to close your eyes or keep your gaze focused on one spot in front of you. Take a few deep breaths and then begin by bringing your attention to your breath as you breathe in. Notice the tip of your nose as your breath enters your body. Continue to breathe normally, following your inhalations as your breath flows down into your lungs. Notice your lungs expand as your breath fills them, and then notice them begin to contract during your exhalations.

- Continue following your breath in this manner for ten minutes. The first few times you practice you may find that much of your time is spent lost in thought rather than focused on your breathing. You may lose focus and bring your attention back many, many times over the course of several minutes. Don't worry, this is part of the practice.

We hope that some of the ideas above can help you deal with the feeling of misfit and prepare you to move forward. Being misfit hurts. Even the most experienced and self-assured individuals can struggle to regain their bearings. Reestablishing a sense of who you are, what you want, and what you're capable of achieving helps to assure you that, whether you stay in your current job or move on, you'll be better equipped to tackle the challenges with a sense of optimism and possibility. Being kind to yourself and taking extra good care of your physical and mental well-being will help prepare you for the better future ahead.

Remember that even if you're misfit in your job, you're still worthy. You still matter, and there's a better fit out there somewhere for you. Stop comparing yourself to others and finding yourself wanting, stop feeling bad that your effort alone can't fix this, and stop waiting until you or the situation are perfect before making a change. Admit misfit, and start doing what you can to fix it!

CHAPTER 15

Flexing to Fit
Where You Are

Flexibility makes buildings to be stronger, imagine what it can do to your soul.

— Carlos Barrios

CERTAIN ELEMENTS OF YOUR JOB are just not working for you right now. You're ready for a change, but not quite ready to quit. We recognize that it's often just not feasible to pack up your office and leave in an instant, fist in the air. A tough economy, family commitments, limited opportunities in your field, financial pressures, and numerous other reasons create situations in which a job change might be unwise. A job search takes time, and when you're searching for a great work fit it can take even longer. Whether you're hoping you might be able to work things out in your current organization, or you need some time to find the right new job, it's possible to make your day-to-day experience better. We call this *flexing to fit*.

When we feel misfit, we often end up on an emotional rollercoaster, experiencing sadness, anger, discouragement, and a feeling that everything is spinning out of control. Before you can change the circumstances, you'll need to try to change your attitude. This is a mind-over-matter approach, and in our experience, for many people, shifting thoughts can powerfully alter perspective and make a poor-fit situation tolerable or, occasionally, much improved. The adage that we can't change other people, but we can adjust our own attitudes and actions, rings very true in misfit work situations. Stephen Covey (1989) championed this notion in his blockbuster book *Seven Habits of Highly Successful People* when he encouraged readers to "focus on what you can control."

Surveys, studies, and research consistently indicate that 85 percent of success in almost any endeavor is dependent on attitude and only 15 percent is dependent on aptitude. If you decide that you're miserable in your job and focus on that fact, then, consciously or unconsciously, you'll do things that reinforce your misery. Alternatively, if you decide that you're willing to flex, you might be able to shift your attitude and some aspects of your performance – and your level of positive fit. We aren't saying to just suck it up, but we are saying that your work may have some good aspects and that you'll feel better if you refocus your attention in that direction. Even if you're in the process of leaving, shifting your thoughts and energy to the few things that may be working well will be a better way to make the transition to a happier future.

That's what happened to Julie, who, 13 years into her career, joined a small, prestigious cosmetics company in a director role. She was particularly excited because of the caliber of the senior leadership team and the quality of the product. Her job was clear and in her sweet spot. She jumped right in. "I couldn't wait to apply what I knew to this challenge."

About four months into the job everything changed. The board brought in new leadership and shifted the direction of the company. "This wasn't what I had signed on for, and I didn't believe it would enable me to learn and expand my skills in the way I had hoped." To make matters worse, the new managers made some significant decisions about quality that Julie felt were inconsistent with her values.

"I recognized that this was probably not the right place for me, but I didn't want to leave so soon after I started. Also, I really liked the team I had hired." To make the best of the situation, Julie focused on the tasks that met the new organizational goals but still provided some learning opportunities for her. "I stuck it out for a year and a half, trying to grow my skills and do the best work I possibly could while keeping my eyes open for another job. I had a lot of frustrating moments, but when the right call came I was ready to move but also able to show an impact from the job I had been in."

Based on the assessments you completed in earlier chapters and your work in Chapter 13, "Calculating the Elements and Weighing Trade-Offs," you should now be aware of which of the work-fit elements feel most misaligned for you and which are most important to work on. Like Julie, it might be about job content and culture, or it might be a change in lifestyle or a difficult relationship with a new boss. Being flexible means bending without breaking. It doesn't mean compromising core values or giving up on your essential requirements for happiness. It simply means taking a step back to reflect on the possibility that making small changes that you can control might make a meaningful difference in how you feel. The following are specific techniques around each of the elements that you can use to flex in ways that will help you survive and, hopefully, move forward to a better work fit.

Flexing to Improve Meaning Fit

For the growing number of employees for whom meaning truly matters, losing your connection to purpose or feeling unseen and disconnected can be one of the most painful misfit experiences. It's difficult to be enthusiastic about work, and very difficult to perform at your best, if you're not sure that what you do matters. While you're unlikely to change the mission of the company, and you may ultimately find that employment with another organization is the right long-term fix, there are strategies for improving your current day-to-day situation.

Remember Why You Took the Job

It's likely that you picked the job you're in because something about it aligned to one or more values that you hold dear. If you feel that you no longer fit in your company, it's possible that you've lost sight of whatever initially drew you to the opportunity. If so, it's probably time to try to reconnect your personal values and your current situation. Spend time reflecting on what was exciting when you first took the job. Try journaling or talking to a friend about what really matters to you and how the job might meet your needs. Evaluate your ability to contribute your best and make a strong impact.

Reconnect to What Matters

Once you've re-examined your core motivations, look for ways to bring them forward in your day-to-day work. It often helps to keep a list of moments that matter. Beth, a geriatric nurse, was struggling with all the frustrating and menial tasks she had to do in her organization. So she decided to focus on what really mattered to her, the fact that she was making a difference in the lives of others, and she savored the value she derived from that. She posted letters from appreciative families in a prominent place in her office to keep this feeling front and center during her day. This helped her feel good that she was doing work that mattered to her rather than feeling frustrated with the job's menial tasks.

Find Out How Your Role Impacts Others

Most of us need to know that what we do matters. Ask your boss or colleagues for feedback on how your work impacts the greater whole. Try to spend time in other areas of the organization so that you can better understand the complete business process. What may seem like a trivial task on the surface may make a big difference to customer satisfaction or to the ability of people in other departments to do their jobs. Inviting others to give you context for why what you do matters can make a huge difference in how you see your role and in your level of motivation.

Consider the Company Mission

Meaning may be found by better understanding and seeking ways to support the company's mission. To help connect your work to the greater good, talk to your boss and others at work about the company's mission and how it matters to the world. Many organizations have foundations that support charitable activities or provide opportunities for community service. Find ways to get involved with these service initiatives.

Look Outside Your Job

When you're struggling with purpose at work, it can be helpful to turn to outside interests. Hobbies or volunteering can fill your need for meaning, and they can also give you more energy to handle the stresses of your job. When Cammie was struggling with being misfit at work but had decided to continue with the company for personal reasons, Moe, in her coaching role, suggested to Cammie that she take part of the energy that she had been pouring into the job and put it into an outside activity. Moe advised that the satisfaction and learning opportunities that would result would actually decrease her sense of frustration from a less-than-perfect job. Cammie got involved with a nonprofit organization that was using art to raise awareness of issues impacting women around the world. She made new friends, learned new skills, and found a sense of purpose that carried over into a more positive attitude during the workday.

Flexing to Improve Job Fit

Job fit can actually be one of the easier elements to flex, especially at larger companies with a variety of positions and opportunities. Most jobs involve a mix of tasks we really enjoy and tasks we simply tolerate or manage to endure. Mike, an administrative assistant, loves to plan offsite meetings and events and handle special projects for his boss, but he dislikes constantly revising calendar appointments. Jude, a financial analyst, gets great satisfaction from creating models and doing forecasts, but she really dislikes negotiating with other functions or sitting in on weekly department meetings. It's normal to dislike some parts of your job. And that's not necessarily a sign that the job or organization is wrong for you.

Our experience with countless employees in a wide variety of roles has shown that it's often possible – and usually helpful – to reshape a job in which you feel misfit by taking on more or fewer tasks, expanding or diminishing the scope of the tasks, or changing how the tasks are performed.

Dissect Your Work

Take time to examine your work carefully, reflecting on all the tasks you do, and consider which ones bring the most enjoyment and which cause the greatest dissatisfaction. Troy was feeling frustrated in his job as an HR recruiter because of his daily tasks. We suggested that he take a look at his job by first listing his tasks and then rating them high, medium, or low for how much time they took, how much he enjoyed them, and how he thought they were perceived by the organization. The results are shown in Figure 15-1.

In looking at his work this way, Troy realized that he was spending a lot of time managing the database of candidates and posting jobs because the technology infrastructure was inadequate for the task. He didn't particularly like the work, but he especially didn't like that it required so much of his time and energy. He wanted to create a better college recruiting program, such as he had done in a previous company, but that

	TROY'S EXAMPLE: EVALUATING CURRENT JOB TASKS		
Job Tasks	Current Time Required	Level of Enjoyment	Organizational Priority
Communicating with Applicants	High	High	High
Looking through Resumes	High	Medium	Medium
Managing Database	High	Low	Medium
Managing Job Postings	High	Low	Medium
Networking	Low	High	Low
Attending Department Meetings	Medium	Medium	Medium
College Recruiting	Low	High	Medium
Meeting with Supervisor	Medium	Medium	Medium
Answering Internal Emails	Medium	Low	Medium
Writing Job Descriptions	High	Low	Low

Figure 15-1. Troy evaluated his job by first listing his tasks and then rating them high, medium, or low for how much time they took, how much he enjoyed them, and how he thought they were perceived by the organization. This reflection helped him break down disconnects between where he was spending time and what he enjoyed doing. The shaded job tasks show areas of misalignment.

wasn't something that his current organization had yet embraced. After doing the exercise, he decided to try to free up time and create more efficiency with his tasks by recommending that the department hire a data entry clerk to be shared across the recruiting organization. Then he built a business case for the benefit of a college recruiting program and offered to take on that responsibility.

We have included a similar exercise in Appendix 4, "Work Relationships Matrix." This type of reflection helps you to break down disconnects between where you're spending time and what you enjoy. Shifting time to the tasks you enjoy can significantly alter your overall sense of satisfaction and purpose.

Create Opportunity for Growth

Lack of job fit is frequently connected to feeling overqualified or to your job lacking in opportunities for growth. This is the time to take your development into your own hands. Talk to your boss about additional assignments or special projects. Sign up for committees or offer to help colleagues.

Ann is a nurse practitioner in an obstetrics-gynecology practice who has learned to create her own opportunities for growth. After several years in the job, she realized that, while she liked the work and her colleagues, the day-to-day tasks had become monotonous. "I wasn't unhappy; it had just become routine and I felt stagnant. Learning new things is important to me." She had heard many of the clinic's patients complaining about sexual dysfunction and found the topic interesting and relevant to some of her previous studies. She decided that she could position herself as the team's expert in this area. She took the initiative to sign up for extra training and attend several conferences, and then she talked to her boss about being the group's specialist. "My boss was 100 percent supportive. He told me to take it as far as I wanted to and that the team would begin pointing to me as the expert. My colleagues have been thrilled to have the additional support. It makes me feel good to be helping them and helping women in the community. It has made me feel much better about my job."

Strengthen Your Skills

Sometimes lack of job fit is connected to a sense of feeling unqualified to perform parts of your job. Feeling anxious about performance is never good. If this applies to you, focus on developing and shoring up your skills. There are many resources available to help you learn and build competence: find online courses in your field, go to a seminar, read more books, or watch inspiring TED talks. Commit time to start growing in your capabilities as a way to counteract any feelings of inadequacy.

Flexing to Improve Culture Fit

Culture fit can be among the most difficult of the work fit elements to flex – it's that invisible force in an organization that defines "how we do things here." Over the long term, it's hard to fundamentally shift your values and personality if they're out of sync with the practices of the organization. If you observe systemic behavior that's inconsistent with your sense of integrity or involves abusive, unethical, or immoral activity, the answer is to leave as quickly as you can (and, in some cases, report transgressions to authorities). In the case of subtler cultural differences, however, it's occasionally possible to improve culture fit, or at least to make adaptations that can enable you to hang on until you find a better opportunity.

Find Like-Minded Colleagues

We've noticed that even in extremely misfit cultural situations clients can usually find a few friends or allies. Having these relationships of trust not only helps you get more accomplished, it also provides moments of joy during long work weeks.

This was a strategy Bob used successfully when he found a lack of fit after taking a new job at a fast-growing software company. "My instincts told me it might not be the right culture, but the role provided an interesting new challenge and the company was growing quickly, so I told myself it was close enough. I should have explored the culture more. I quickly found that it was quite different from the well-established leading company where I had previously worked. More like the wild, wild west. There was lots of after-hours socializing and drinking. No manuals, no training, lack of any process. I lasted a year by focusing on building relationships and a good coalition with a group of more like-minded people, including the head of sales. I aligned myself with those people and then just focused on getting things done where I could and trying to get satisfaction from those moments while I looked for my next opportunity. I still count those allies as key friends and an important part of my network."

Identify Behaviors That Might Be Causing Friction

Consider that some of your actions might be creating stress between you, your coworkers, and the organization you work for. When possible, view the behaviors not as right or wrong but simply as differences. For example, you might want to be trusted to make decisions on your own, but the organization requires a lot of consensus and data. Without fundamentally changing your independence, how can you embrace the value of consensus for now? Or can you attempt to discuss the differences with colleagues and your boss to strike a compromise?

Elizabeth was brought into a new company to create change in the organization. She quickly discovered that the culture was not a great fit. "The organization wasn't very open to new ways of doing things. To make it more difficult, my boss, the CEO, was very introverted and not really focused on relationships. I wasn't able to get much help from him. I had a financial need to stay, so I decided to try to make it work as long as I could. My nature is hard-charging and results-driven. I realized that I would need to be very collaborative and less territorial than might be my nature. I saw that I needed to build relationships and earn people's trust." Eventually, Elizabeth was able to make an impact on the business results. "Toward the end of my first year, we had a big internal meeting. When I saw the work that I had done being presented, I felt like 'oh my gosh, pinch me, what I wanted to see happen is happening. I'm making a transformational impact.'"

Consider Style or Communication Adjustments

While you can't easily change your natural working tendencies to fit a misaligned culture, you can become more conscious of how your behavior impacts others and make appropriate adjustments in order to make work more comfortable, satisfying, and productive. Assessment tools that we referred to in Chapter 12, "Knowing Yourself and What You Want," such as Everything DiSC, Leadership Practices Inventory, and Strengths Finder, frequently include specific recommendations for how to better engage with people who have different work styles. Many of their suggestions can also be applied to adjusting to better fit with an organization's culture. Developing new skills or modifying your approach can help to make interactions easier, which in turn can lead to less strain at work and better performance.

Elizabeth was able to flex in ways that made her original culture misfit manageable for the long term. For Bob, the presence of both style and values differences meant minimizing pain during the time it took to find a better job. Consider how you might flex, without compromising your values, in order to feel more comfortable and productive in a culture that's not a natural fit.

Flexing to Improve Relationship Fit
with Colleagues

As we noted in Chapter 6, "Relationship Fit," our relationships at work are among the most critical factors of our job satisfaction. When those relationships are broken, we often feel misfit. Healthy relationships at work take effort to develop.

Analyze Your Relationships Objectively

It's all too easy when you feel misfit at work to bring confirmation bias to every interaction. Even one bad relationship can impact your perception of your workplace if you allow it to happen. Try to set aside emotion and look impartially at all your individual relationships to get at the source of your frustration.

Get to Know Your Colleagues

The more you know someone, the more likely you are to find common ground. Ask colleagues to have coffee with you without any agenda beyond learning their story and sharing yours (be explicit about wanting to get to know them better for work). Listen to their needs and motivations at work. Focus on listening to understand them rather than first being understood. Try to find at least one common connection or interest.

Be Willing to Be Vulnerable

As Patrick Lencioni (2003) discusses in his book *The Five Dysfunctions of a Team,* openness about weaknesses and mistakes builds trust and cohesion. Try modeling this behavior. Be open and honest about your strengths, concerns, and vulnerabilities. Share a misstep with your colleagues openly and with humility.

Learn to Navigate Conflict

Develop fluency in having hard conversations and practice embracing conflict. The Harvard Negotiation Project offers many resources that will help you, such as their book *Difficult Conversations: How to Discuss What Matters Most* (Stone, Patton, and Heen 1999) and *Crucial Conversations: Tools for Talking when the Stakes are High* (Patterson et al. 2011).

Seek Out Like-Minded Colleagues

When you're dealing with a difficult coworker, it helps to balance out the bad by seeking out the good. Look for people in the organization who share your passions and interests. You might find them through volunteering for activities with groups outside your department. It might help to become part of extracurricular work activities, such as the company softball team or a diversity network, so that you can meet new colleagues and make new connections. Having someone you look forward to going to lunch with can also make a major difference in your daily motivation and satisfaction.

Practice Empathy

Empathy is the ability to feel with and understand another. Nursing scholar Theresa Wiseman (2015) describes the practice of empathy as having four steps:

- See the world as others see it.
- Be nonjudgmental.
- Understand others' feelings.
- Communicate your understanding of others' feelings.

Empathy facilitates positive connection with others because, in the face of their human struggles, we can authentically convey "me too."

Kim worked as a coordinator in an events-planning company. One coworker, Jane, was really challenging. Kim frequently felt that Jane was attacking her projects in front of other colleagues and their boss. Under attack, Kim began to have the feeling that everyone in her work group undervalued her contributions, and she suspected that people were talking about her behind her back. Whenever a colleague hesitated, or gave her critical feedback, she assumed that "this is happening because they just don't like me," and she frequently complained about other employees to members of the team. Kim's reaction wasn't productive or healthy – for herself or for her team. Poor behavior like Kim's can cause further alienation in a tough work-fit scenario and create feelings of isolation and loneliness. When Kim evaluated the situation objectively, she recognized that her negative feelings were stemming primarily from this one colleague. She also recognized that the level of interaction was actually low and that this colleague had no experience in her job area. She also remembered that Jane had recently gone through a difficult divorce. To try to build some trust between them, she decided to set up a meeting to provide more background on what she and her team were currently working on. She hoped that increasing her colleague's awareness of the group's work would lead to better understanding and less criticism.

Being a good team member means bringing your best interpersonal skills to the table to create healthy, cohesive relationships that will help you to feel connected and like you belong.

In Appendix 4, "Work Relationships Matrix," we have a framework that helped Kim think more objectively about her relationships at work. Try filling out the matrix for yourself. List important relationships (your boss, colleagues, and people who work for you). For each relationship, consider which colleagues are important to you in your role. Look also at those with whom you have low frequency of interaction, trust, or social comfort. Consider how you might invest in these relationships to improve the connection and partnership.

Flexing to Improve Relationship Fit with Your Boss

While dealing with difficult coworkers can be exhausting, misfit with your direct supervisor can be almost unbearable. As one of our friends says, "The boss is the culture." Here are ideas we've seen garner the most success for employees suffering misfit due primarily to their boss.

Speak Up

Consider respectfully and in private giving your boss feedback about the impact they have on you. It's possible that they haven't received meaningful, direct feedback about their behavior from others, and that's why their poor managerial behaviors continue. You need to have that difficult conversation with your boss that lets them know why you're struggling together and what you hope for in the future?

Ask For What You Need

It's highly likely that, in an effort to prove your own competence, you've locked up any needs you have, so that from the outside looking in you're a rugged individualist. But when you're feeling poor fit in your job, before you go you owe it to yourself to give every effort you can, including an honest and open ask about what you need, in order to be at your best. Marshall Goldsmith says, "We abuse self-sufficiency, ignoring the value of a supportive environment, taking foolish pride in doing it all ourselves. We trigger our isolation."

Reflect on Why Your Boss is Pushing Your Buttons

Consider how you might be contributing to the situation. As we discussed before, certain people may just rub us the wrong way. Steve is, by his own admission, overly concerned about order and tidiness. So when his boss appears to be less tidy or orderly, Steve judges him harshly and gets annoyed. While the boss's behavior may be imperfect, the person with the issue and frustration is Steve, due to his expectations and personal habits. Learning to accept the imperfections of other people will help Steve see his boss in a more comprehensive light, with less judgment and, therefore, less frustration.

Get Clear On Your Boss's Expectations

Misaligned or murky work expectations are a leading cause of frustration for employees who are unhappy with their boss. Spend time probing and clarifying with your boss what exactly they're looking for so that you, and they, can be satisfied that you meet the mark.

Practice Empathy

Can you try on your boss's perspective without judging them? Can you use empathy to more deeply understand where they're coming from in order to build genuine feeling for the world from their view? This may foster a more authentic connection between you.

If these strategies don't improve your situation, and you enjoy other aspects of your work or the company, one of the most common strategies you can employ is to try to find work in another part of the organization. This is particularly effective if you've been with the organization long enough to have developed good relationships with employees in other departments.

This was the case with Rebecca. She worked for a large corporation that had several offices, and she had requested a move to the California office because of a personal need. The new boss was quite difficult and made it clear that Rebecca wasn't the person he wanted for the job, even telling her that he really wanted to take another person but was forced to take her. She had evidently failed to respond quickly enough to a request he had made when she was in a previous role, and she was still on his "bad person list." "I was sitting in his office, pregnant with my oldest, being yelled at. My first thought was, 'Oh no, I just moved and I have to get out of here.'" She reached out to a trusted advisor whom she knew could be trusted with a plan to have her job moved to another group. Fortunately, this worked. She was able to move, and made it look like the idea came from elsewhere.

In particularly difficult situations where a boss-employee relationship has deteriorated, it's important to document interactions and be prepared to voice concerns and solutions – first directly to the boss, and then to HR or others in the organization if the issues aren't addressed.

Ultimately, you want to act like the leader that you wish the boss would be. Working for a bad boss can be a great way to sharpen your understanding of your own values and how you want to interact with others.

Flexing to Improve Lifestyle Fit

Misfit between work and outside responsibilities can be extremely painful and feel especially difficult to address. Many of us perceive a stigma around revealing our outside priorities. "Will they think I'm not dedicated? Will I be penalized in my performance review?" Because lifestyle misfit frequently happens with a change in our personal situation, it can be daunting to shift behavior or ask for a change in work circumstances that were previously not an issue.

For many clients, a lifestyle misfit has eventually led to a change in employer or job to one that better met their personal needs. But before you assume that you need to make that change, it's worth considering opportunities to flex within your current situation.

Honestly Assess What You Need

Thoughtfully consider what you need and/or desire right now for better balance in your life. Think about the specifics of what would be helpful. Ideas that we've seen work include:

- Tighter boundaries between work and personal time (e.g., less pressure to answer emails or phone calls after hours)
- An opportunity to work from home (How many days would make a difference?)
- Reduced hours

- A change in schedule (e.g., starting and leaving earlier or a compressed four-day workweek)
- Time off to take care of personal needs (Vacation? Sabbatical? Personal leave?)

Do Your Homework

Are there examples within your work group or in the company that appear to be working for others that might work for you? It can be useful to talk to HR about policies and appropriate working styles that already exist in your company as well as lessons they've learned on what's worked for others and what hasn't.

Create a Proposal

Talk to your boss about a specific plan for how you might improve your lifestyle fit and still deliver value to the company. Remember to communicate how your plan can be beneficial to the employer – don't just focus on your own needs. Listen carefully to your boss's perspective and concerns. If your boss is extremely hesitant, propose a trial period so that you can both evaluate how the plan is working. Agree on success metrics, and show that you can outperform those metrics in the ways that are important.

Practice Self-Care

Getting a good night's sleep, exercising, and eating right are frequently cast aside when we're under the stress of juggling too many responsibilities. Find out if your employer has an employee assistance program and consider using its services to talk to a counselor.

Learn to Say No

To improve your balance, it's critical that you ruthlessly prioritize outside commitments and learn to say no. Brian Andreas, the innovative author and illustrator of *Story People,* says it well: "Everything changed the day she figured out there was exactly enough time for the important things in her life."

Bella had worked for a bank for many years in customer service. She loved the people and the job, so when her husband retired and wanted to move two hours away, she felt torn. Bella wasn't opposed to some commuting, and she had family she could stay with, so she approached her boss and asked to work a compressed schedule of 40 hours in three days. She prepared for the conversation, built her case, and made it clear that she wanted to stay but had to have more flexibility. Her boss suggested instead that they try having her work from her new home three days a week and commute to the office two days. This type of arrangement had never been done, and it required both new technical support from the bank and new behaviors from Bella and her colleagues, who weren't used to a remote work situation. In Bella's words, "I was nervous about what people would think, and it took some adjustment, but it has worked out great. The trust that I had built over the years really paid off. I'm so glad that I spoke up and asked for what I needed rather than just assumed that I needed to quit."

Flexing to Improve Financial Fit

Most of us would like a bigger paycheck. It's easy to mentally spend an extra 10 percent on things that feel like they would improve our lives! But financial misfit isn't just about desiring more pay, it's about feeling that we're not being appropriately compensated for the work we're doing or that our work is not paying enough to meet our basic needs.

Kathy joined her company as the HR manager of one manufacturing plant. Over a three-year period, the scope of her job increased as she secured HR managers at four different plants, elevating her to the role of director, in which she oversaw people development company-wide. She was given a standard pay increase annually, but when she benchmarked her salary using PayScale, she realized that while the scope of her job had increased significantly, as had her responsibilities, her pay had not. After some careful preparation, Kathy approached her boss with data and an open mind. "I was nervous about talking to them, since I had grown with the company and felt worried it was 'not my place' to demand a higher salary. At the same time, I wanted to be compensated fairly relative to my peers, and I felt the pressures of the higher position." Her boss appreciated the benchmarking data and agreed that her salary should increase commensurate with her responsibility, and they crafted a staged plan to raise it substantially to match her title of director. Kathy felt seen and valued after her pay was increased, and she's able to continue in her role feeling that she's respected and treated fairly.

Here are some tips for how you might negotiate if, like Kathy, you feel that you're not being properly compensated for your work.

Stay Objective and Check the Facts

In our experience, it's critical to manage the almost inevitable anger that accompanies feeling underpaid. Do some honest assessment: do you have the same experience, responsibility, and skill set as your colleagues, who you believe are making more?

Prepare a List of Your Accomplishments

Reflect on and document what you've achieved in your job: money saved, customers satisfied, people managed, revenue created, sales closed.

Practice the Conversation

Having a conversation about not being properly compensated for your work can be difficult and emotional. Before tackling it "for real," try practicing on a trusted friend or colleague. This will help you refine your communication and present your case in the most effective fashion.

Bring Your Concerns to Your Boss

When you talk to your boss, avoid the kind of confrontational stance that will put them on the defensive. Communicate confidently but in a way that shows your commitment to the company and to achieving goals together. Acknowledge that you understand that there are a lot of different factors that go into determining salary, but that you've recently found some information that causes you concern. Approach the conversation as a request for information, feedback, and understanding rather than as a firm request for a raise.

Be Thoughtful About Timing

While it may seem natural to bring up financial concerns during your annual review, it may actually be better to do it before the formal review process begins. The discussion can be especially appropriate after you successfully complete a major project or when you're asked to take on additional responsibilities.

Consider Other Forms of "Pay"

As an alternative to asking for a salary increase, think about additional currencies such as more vacation, additional training, or a bonus. These may be easier for your boss to approve and will help to address your sense of inequity.

No for Now

If the answer is "no" – consider taking it as "no for now" and ask what it might take to get to a future "yes."

If your feelings of financial misfit are stemming from financial need rather than a sense of inequity, you'll likely need a longer-term approach. Talk to your boss about additional training or skills that can increase your value to the company. Investigate opportunities to gain certifications or build skills through local education programs or online classes. And in the meantime, try to reduce spending on non-essentials so that your pay and your financial requirements are a better match.

Create a Flex Action Plan

While you might have a long list of ways that you don't fit in your company, don't try to change too many things at once. Gradual change will be easier for you to accomplish and less likely to be met with suspicion or opposition from others. Think about breaking in new behavior just as you would break in a new pair of shoes.

After developing a list of possible actions, reflect on the ones that feel like an expansion of who you are rather than a departure. This can become a time to develop new skills that can help you even outside of work relationships. You might sign up for a training class, ask your boss for more specific feedback on development opportunities, improve a relationship with a difficult colleague, or ask for flexibility to shift your schedule.

ASK YOURSELF . . .

- Am I truly committed to putting the time and energy into changing my behavior?
- Can I do so in a way that's not detrimental to my fundamental character and strengths?
- If I change this area, will I be more effective in my role?

It's easier to change behavior when you set clear and specific goals. For example, "I will be more innovative" is too general and much less likely to be accomplished than "For the next three months I will read a newsletter in my industry every week and write down an idea my department could leverage." Goals should be clear, specific, and measurable. They also should be important to you as well as something you can commit to accomplishing.

Recognize your limitations and be honest about whether the payoff is worth the effort to make the change, or whether it's simply too inconsistent with your natural style and desires.

Creating a written plan with goals and milestones will be an important and effective way to track progress and ensure that you're headed in the right direction. Also, flexing is hard work and will require a strong support system. You are much more likely to be successful if you cultivate relationships with trusted people who can provide feedback and who can also help you to stay objective about just how far you want to go to try to fit in.

Your boss can be an important ally, particularly if you can frame your goals as part of a development plan to make you more effective at your job. Your boss can provide ongoing assessment and feedback by directly observing your behavior. For example, you might struggle with the need to spend large amounts of time gaining consensus from colleagues in other departments and prefer a more autonomous environment. Your boss, who knows that developing relationships with these colleagues will benefit you and the organization, can see that you're given help in improving your consensus-building skills and provide an ongoing assessment of your improvement.

A trusted mentor or coach is an ideal partner with whom you can be honest about your full situation – both your commitment to make changes and your concerns about the ultimate fit. They can help hold you accountable as you try new skills and behaviors.

It's also important to confide in a trusted friend or family member and solicit their emotional support. Fitting a round peg in a square hole can be exhausting. It helps to have someone who can provide moral support and encouragement and who will recognize your achievements along the way.

FLEX PLAN TEMPLATE	
Goal	What element do I want to flex?
Action Steps	What will I do differently to reach this goal?
	What specific people can help me make this change?
	How can I ask for help?
	What are some of the challenges that I'll face?
	How might I overcome these challenges?
Benefit	What benefit will I gain if I make this change?

Figure 15-2. Use this template to create your own flex plan.

The template in Figure 15-2 will help you create an effective flex plan.

Focusing on those aspects of the job that are fully within your control, such as rebuilding your confidence, reconnecting to what matters to you, improving relationships, and recrafting tasks, is a logical starting point when you feel misfit at work but aren't ready or able to make a job change quickly. Many people have expressed to us that by using the ideas described in this chapter, they were frequently able to stay in their jobs longer than they expected, reduced stress related to poor fit, and, in many cases, created long-term satisfaction that resulted, over time, in a positive fit for them in their companies.

CHAPTER 16

Deciding to Leave and Going Gracefully

Call it what you will, but quitting a strategy, or a job, should not be seen as failure. We can't win at everything we do.

— Robert Herjavec

THERE COMES A POINT when you just have to admit that it's time to go. Maybe you've tried to adjust your style, your perspective, and your job tasks and you're still misfit. Maybe the pain of being in the wrong place or working for the wrong person has finally outweighed the commitment you feel to your colleagues or team. Maybe you can no longer deny that the job is negatively affecting your health or personal relationships. For whatever reason, there's a time to simply say this job isn't a good fit for me, I can't change that, and it's time to move on.

For some people, the decision to leave can be reached fairly easily. We've talked to clients who enjoyed aspects of their jobs and valued the relationships with their teams or peers but lacked the opportunity to grow. When a job with more attractive prospects came up it was a no-brainer for them to make the switch. Often, they did so with the blessings of their boss and colleagues. Clients who didn't feel a strong connection at work were quick to jump on what felt like a better financial or lifestyle fit. We've also seen people who were so miserable, usually because of deep culture misfit, that they simply felt they had no choice but to go and go fast.

More often, however, individuals who recognize that it's time to move on find it difficult to make the change. There can be tangible obstacles such as geographic and financial constraints. But often the reasons are more emotional. In some cases, these individuals are in prestigious organizations and feel like they'll lose credibility if they exit. This is particularly true if the realization of misfit comes early and they fear being labeled as job-hoppers or fear leaving without achieving measurable results. It can be difficult, especially for high achievers, to admit that the job's not working. Quitting can feel like giving up rather than moving on. There may be pressure from friends or family to stick it out. Sometimes people begin to think that the problem is with them rather than with the organization. Mario said, "It was guilt inducing. I felt incompetent and as though I had failed. It impacted me greatly."

We've seen many people who convince themselves that their misfit situation is normal – or at least that it's as good as it gets. A clear sign that this may be happening is when you find yourself responding to inquiries about how work is going with phrases like "Well, nobody really likes their job, do they?" or "I guess my job is no worse than anybody else's." Even bad situations can feel more comfortable than the discomfort associated with looking for a new job or being out of work. Aidan said it this way: "It's always stressful to feel that you're giving up on anything . . . as well as quitting a company. And there's so much that's terrifying in the unknowns."

Many times we've seen people stay in painful situations because they have a strong sense of loyalty to their teams or colleagues. This can be especially true if they've recruited other people into the company. Moving on can bring about tremendous feelings of guilt if we feel like we're abandoning people we care about. We feel guilty for "jumping ship." Daniel Gulati, co-author of *Passion and Purpose,* suggests that even people in gravely unsatisfying jobs don't quit because of a tendency to overthink decisions, fear eventual failure, and prioritize near-term, visible rewards over long-range success (Coleman 2012, Gladding 2011, Gray 1999, Pychyl 2009).

Acknowledging that you're in pain is hard. Taking action to change your circumstances can be even harder. It may help to recognize that over the course of your working life you're likely to switch jobs multiple times. Sometimes it may be due to misfit and sometimes to better opportunities or changes in your personal or professional goals. This isn't a new trend. The average employee in their 50s has already held 11.7 jobs (U.S. Department of Labor 2015). And the Millennial generation is poised to change jobs even more frequently, largely in pursuit of better fit. If you've decided that the best option is a work change, resist the temptation to feel bad about going. Remember that it's a natural part of the evolution of your work life. Focus on the chance to use your experience and earned wisdom for a more fulfilling job.

In his job as a web designer with a startup, Aaron faced the challenge of admitting it was time to go. "My first experience with work misfit reminded me of an unhealthy relationship. I knew some major things were wrong, but I kept telling myself that the (dwindling) things that were going right would somehow be enough. At the time, I didn't have a clear enough understanding of how my values related to work, so there was no way to measure the current experience against other possibilities. I told myself that it must be grass-is-greener thinking, and I stayed about two years longer than I should have. Leaving the company was a leap of faith and (eventually) a confidence builder. About a year after the move, I was able to effectively retrospect on my previous job and my personal values. I found that I learned just as much about myself and what I need as I did about why that wasn't the right fit for me."

Quitting Well

Quitting well takes a combination of courage and honest self-assessment. We found that it's helpful to balance your emotions with tools and outside perspectives that will help you to think objectively about your situation. Here are some ideas that have been helpful to others.

Take a Self-Assessment

Consider taking an assessment such as the one that we have included in Appendix 5, "Is It Time to Leave? Assessment" from Amy Wrzesniewski, Professor of Organizational Behavior at the Yale School of Management. Her research explores how people make meaning of their work, with a focus on the impact that meaning has on employees and the organizations in which they work. Doing this type of exercise can help you to break through stories you may be telling yourself about the need to stay and lead you to a better understanding of the reality you're facing.

Seek an Outside Perspective

Find a confidante outside of work who can serve as a sounding board. Sharing your feelings out loud will likely give you a new perspective, and a friend can give you an honest assessment of how the situation is affecting you. You may also earn their support for the journey ahead.

Envision the Future

Visualize yourself giving notice. How does it make you feel? One client calls it the stomach test. If you start to feel sick and anxious, then you might have some more work to do before you're ready to leave. If you feel a sense of relief and joy, then it's obviously time to move on.

Re-examine Your Circumstances

Reality-check the specifics of your situation. By talking to others and assessing yourself objectively you can gain perspective on how serious the situation is for you right now. This frequently necessitates some difficult conversations, possibly with your boss.

This was the case with Rebecca, who found herself needing to confront her boss. "I had never had a bad relationship with a boss before – really ever, which is kind of amazing because I've had a 20-plus-year career. But at this job, no matter what I did, I felt that my boss held me in disdain and barely tolerated my feeble attempts at managing my team in a direction he wanted to go. Added to this was a crushing commute that consumed over two hours of my day. I finally worked up the courage to confront my boss and tell him how unhappy I was. I told him I was at a fork in the road, and if he and the company really didn't value my contribution, I needed to leave. If they did actually value my talent, then I needed to better understand what I was doing right because everything I did seemed like it was wrong in their eyes (though I was personally very proud of my team's and my accomplishments). He ultimately came back and fired me with a severance package. Though I was surprised at first, on the day that I left the building I felt immense relief. I would almost call it giddy. I don't think I really understood how unhappy I was until I was released from that toxic environment. Even though I had no job lined up, which would normally have stressed me out, I felt like God had given me a gift and a huge blessing. It took me a few months to re-center myself since the whole experience had challenged my paradigm about myself. I believed that I was competent, talented, and could be successful in any environment – as I had proven over and over earlier in my career. What it taught me was that sometimes, no matter how hard you try, you may be in an environment where you just don't fit, and it's no one's fault necessarily . . . but that doesn't mean you should stay there. I won't hang on so long if there's a next time."

ASK YOURSELF . . .

- What indications do I have that it's time to exit?
- What might be holding me back?
- How might I get more comfortable with the decision to leave?

Making Your Exit

Regardless of the circumstances around your departure, there are things you can do to leave with as much assurance and dignity as possible.

Prepare Yourself

As soon as you make the decision to leave, start marketing yourself for your next opportunity. Through the work you've done in earlier chapters, especially Chapter 12, "Knowing Yourself and What You Want," you should have a good sense of the type of job and organization that will be the best match and provide the most satisfaction for you. As you polish your resume and LinkedIn profile, emphasize the experiences and skills that have brought you fulfillment. Use the strategies in Chapter 17, "Evaluating New Opportunities," to identify the companies that look to be a good match, and start to network with employees at these companies. While it's important to expand your network, be selective about who you talk with about your search. You don't want a difficult situation in your current job to get even tenser because people know that you're looking.

Leave Toward Something

According to career experts, it's much easier to find a new job when you're still employed. It's also much easier to explain a move when you can share a specific new opportunity with your old boss and company. But that's not always possible. Sometimes you need to leave even when you don't know what's happening next.

Even without your next job lined up, it's possible to leave toward something and to have a message for your current colleagues that will be respected and understood. Explain that your passions and interests are pulling you in a new direction. Many organizations appreciate hearing that you don't want to give less than your best while you're looking for a new opportunity. Keep your comments positive, try to express gratitude for what the company has done for you, and acknowledge the personal learning or growth you experienced (there's always learning, even in tough or stagnant environments). If you have an opportunity to do an exit interview, tell the truth about your experience and issues with the boss, culture, compensation, etc. in order to help the company learn. But keep your tone as positive and helpful as possible.

Go with Grace

When the time comes to share the news of your leaving, strive to maintain positive relationships with those in your current company. Explain your reasoning and try to help make the transition easy. This means no slamming doors on the way out. Remember that even in misfit situations there are likely to be relationships that you'll want to maintain. We've heard countless stories of connections that resurfaced elsewhere that were helpful.

Ensure a Smooth Transition

Give everyone adequate time to prepare for your departure. Two weeks is often not enough notice. Senior roles require three to four weeks' notice. Try to finish up projects where possible and leave detailed notes to help the person who will be taking on your responsibilities. Offer your replacement or former team the opportunity to reach out if they need help. If they welcome your help, check in with your replacement once a week until you're not needed anymore.

Exiting was a long process of for Barb. She had been unhappy with her relationship with her boss for more than a year because of their very different work styles. But when she at last secured a job that felt like a better fit, it was high season at her job. She didn't want to leave her employer in the lurch, so she agreed to stay on until they could hire her replacement. She was able to overlap a few weeks in order to start her replacement's training, despite her eagerness to start her new role. Her new job, fundraising at a nonprofit, required interfacing with many of the same people she worked with at her old job, so Barb worked hard to exit with grace. She never spoke poorly about her boss, and she actively maintained positive relationships even after she left. Both companies were delighted with her work, even the one she left. Her patience, calm, and empathy for the challenges left in her wake at her former employer facilitated an open and positive exit. "To this day, I feel pride in how I left. I'm happy that despite the challenges I worked hard to keep my actions and my attitude positive."

ASK YOURSELF . . .

- What would a positive transition look like for me?
- What steps can I take to ensure a graceful exit?

Leaving a job, particularly one you had high hopes for, can be draining. It's like giving up a dream or a bit of yourself. But time and time again what we hear from people who have taken that step is a sense of relief and the seeds of new joy:

- *Leaving the job felt like a breath of fresh air, a huge weight lifted off my shoulders, and a step in the right direction to pursuing my dreams.*

- *When it's a misfit, you dread the thought of going to work. I didn't like feeling like a quitter when I left. Afterwards, though, it felt like a giant weight had been lifted from my shoulders.*

- *Accepting that things were not going to change, and that I could not succeed within that environment, was a long and painful process. Leaving was such an incredible relief.*

- *It was exhilarating, a huge stress relief – seemed like I saved myself ten extra years to live.*

- *It feels like a new beginning, and I'm planning for new opportunities down the road.*

- *It was a huge relief to feel like I could be myself again.*

- *Leaving was like breaking open from a cage and seeing the sun again.*

Could one of these voices be yours?

CHAPTER 17

Evaluating New Opportunities

When you make a choice, you change the future.

— Deepak Chopra

O NCE YOU'VE DECIDED that at this time in your life you're in a job situation that's a poor work fit for you, it's time to begin evaluating other companies and opportunities. It's time to ask yourself, "Where do I want to work next?" This seemingly easy task is, in reality, fraught with difficulties.

Susan said, "Everything looked great from the outside. I took the job and within two weeks I knew it was a bad fit. My boss was dishonest about how things were really done at the company, which was so disappointing because I had left a job I loved. It took five months, but I did leave. I hope that for my next job I'll be better able to assess what I'm getting into before I say yes." Things can look very, very different from the outside of an organization from what they actually are on the inside.

So how can you realistically assess whether a job or company you're considering is going to be a great work fit for you, when all you have to go on is initial impressions from the interview process?

Key Actions for Evaluating Opportunities

Assuming that you've cultivated a short list of opportunities based on companies interested in you, industry or role choices that fit well for you, or places you have a likelihood of an interview, we suggest that you spend time on four key actions to increase the likelihood of finding a good fit for yourself.

Know What Work-Fit Elements Help You Thrive

Spend time, before you look at organizations, looking at yourself. What do you know about yourself that might make a difference in the culture fit for a particular company? Remember the values you identified in Chapter 12, "Knowing Yourself and What You Want"? We like to think of these as guiding lights that show you what you hold dear. If you land at a company that doesn't consider a value of yours important, or at least relevant, you'll likely feel misfit. While personal values are different from professed organizational values and serve a different purpose, the clearer you can be about the dimensions of work that you value highly, the more likely you'll be able to look at a company with open eyes. As Brené Brown says, "A value is a way of being or believing that you hold most important."

Do Your Homework

In today's digital age there's a lot of information about every organization available on the web. Do yourself a favor and read everything you can about the one's you're considering. Scour their websites to see what they say about themselves. Some companies with positive employer brands, such as Prudential (make sure to look at their careers page about fit) and Zappos (check out their incredible culture book), offer a plethora of interesting and telling information about themselves. Notice the story that unfolds for you as you read what they say about themselves and what others say about them. Read their blogs, watch their videos, and listen to the threads. Go to employment websites such as glassdoor.com and read what candidates say about them.

ASK YOURSELF . . .

- What vibe do I get about what it's like to work there every day?
- What are their stated values, and how do they synch with what matters to me?
- What unwritten rules does their messaging imply to me?

Talk to People

Once you land an interview, prepare a list of questions that will reveal the often invisible and undiscussed elements of an organization that really matter to fit. In addition, think about people you might talk to about the company, separate from the interview process – casual acquaintances, vendors you may know, recruiters, past employees, and others who may have experience with the company you're considering.

Henry was considering joining a small software company, and as he went through interviews he learned of a few employees whom he knew socially in his community through kid events. He called them, asked them out for coffee, and spent time understanding what the company culture looked like from their points of view. Henry came to the get-togethers prepared with two or three good questions, but he spent most of the time simply listening to the stories that his acquaintances told him about the company. After talking to several people, he noticed threads that mattered to him. The company valued family time, and people flexed their hours accordingly. The executive team reportedly spoke freely and frequently to employees in open meeting spaces rather than in closed rooms. And performance reviews consisted of regular, two-way conversations between boss and employee about progress, goals, and personal dreams. Henry also discovered that people brought dogs to work, which, as a non-dog owner, he wasn't sure about, but the observation intrigued him.

Ask the Right Questions

In your conversations with people you meet in the job process, as well as associates you may know from community, trade, or vendor relationships, the right questions make all the difference. Author Peter Block (2009) says, "The best questions are highly personal and deeply ambiguous." This is never more true than when you're attempting to assess an organization from the outside. You need to get people talking about the company, telling stories that help you get a window on, as well as a visceral experience of, what it's *really* like to work there. These stories will help you to determine whether this is a place for you. One-word answers or yes/no questions won't do this for you. (For sample starter questions by category, see Appendix 6, "Questions to Ask.")

A Note About Company Ratings/Surveys

In the last 20-plus years, there has been a proliferation of best/great-places-to-work surveys hosted by third-party organizations, often media outlets. The phenomenon now known as Great Places to Work (see greatplacetowork.com) was launched by Robert Levering in his 1984 book *100 Best Companies to Work For*, and the list started appearing in *Fortune* magazine in 1997. There are now numerous surveys hosted by media outlets and recruiting companies such as Glassdoor, Gallup, *Business Week, Fortune*, and *Outside Magazine*, as well as specialized and local newspapers and magazines (Schwartz 2011). These surveys are often voluntary, and companies participate based on employee responses, receiving results and rankings after the initial survey. Each particular survey measures workplaces in a slightly different way. For example, according to Levering, "A great place to work is one in which you trust the people you work for, have pride in what you do, and enjoy the people you work with."

Tony Schwartz (2011), author and president of The Energy Project, defines twelve attributes of a truly great place to work in his *Harvard Business Review* article:

1. Pays a living wage

2. All employees have a stake in the company's success

3. Safe, comfortable, and appealing work spaces

4. Healthy, high-quality food at the lowest possible price

5. Places for employees to rest and renew throughout the day

6. Ways for employees to move and stay fit

7. Clear and succinct expectations of what success looks like

8. Two-way performance reviews

9. Managers and leaders who are accountable

10. Time to think and focus

11. Opportunities to learn

12. Stands for something beyond profits

And researchers from Gallup (Flade, Harter, and Asplund 2014) report that there are seven things that great employers do that others don't:

1. Have involved and curious leaders who want to improve.

2. Have cracking HR functions.

3. Ensure that the basic engagement requirements are met before expecting an inspiring mission to matter.

4. Never use a downturn as an excuse.

5. Trust, hold accountable, and relentlessly support managers and teams.

6. Have a straightforward and decisive approach to performance management.

7. Don't pursue engagement for its own sake.

The Gallup researchers go on to say, "Our research in more than 160 countries shows that a job has the potential to be at the heart of a great life, but only if its holder is engaged at work."

There are hundreds of employee motivation, engagement, and morale assessments on the market that are designed to assess various aspects of employee mindset, satisfaction, and connection to the organization. Many of these serve largely as comparative marketing assessments meant to attract candidates to one company over another. Some of these are highly susceptible to temporal changes such as bonuses given or leadership changes. We believe that employee engagement arises out of culture and not the other way around. Falling in love with a company because of a glossy magazine story about them is not the same thing as feeling content there day in and day out.

So, with all this data about what makes a company a great place to work, what's a job seeker to do? Resist the urge to imagine yourself at a company with high ratings on a comparison survey without doing your due diligence to understand the actual culture and it's appropriateness for you. What matters is whether you can tell if a company is a great place for you to work, which is ultimately impossible to discern from surveys or magazine rankings. To assess work fit from the outside requires you to take your research and discovery to new heights as you attempt to uncover whether an organization will be right for you, at this time, and why.

Three Actions to Assess Work Fit

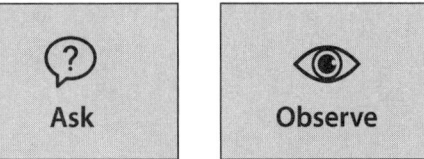

| Research | Ask | Observe |

Figure 17-1. Three key actions will help you assess your potential work fit with a new organization.

We suggest three key actions to help you assess work fit from outside the organization: *research, ask,* and *observe.*

Research – You can research via the Internet, the media, and the public story the company itself publishes on social media and in annual reports, blogs, and internal documents such as employee handbooks. The onus is on you to act like a private investigator to find any and all relevant information on a prospective employer that can tell you what it's like to work there, and whether it's a great fit for you. The advent of digital and social media means that you can source a great deal of unsanctioned feedback about a company by reading what employees and others say online. When Trish was researching jobs, she scoured Facebook for evidence that the people she knew who worked there were unhappy, and pleasantly discovered no evidence in their day-to-day comments.

Ask – The ask process embodies the specific and powerful questions you should ask people you meet at the company through the selection process, as well as people you know who may have a connection to the company. The best questions are ambiguous and personal and reveal nuanced information about "what it's like around here," information that's essential to your consideration of how well you'll fit if you land there. When Marci asked a prospective organization about its flextime policy, she learned that, while they had a written policy, less than 1 percent of employees actually used it, a red flag for the potential to actually flex her schedule.

Observe – Observing an organization involves vigilant and thoughtful attention to how their employees interact with you as a candidate, with their customers, and with their vendors. The best indicator of what a company really values is how the people who work there behave in daily tasks. Observation is even more important than what the organization espouses in its formal communications. When Mac was considering applying to Les Schwab Tire Centers, he decided to go there as a customer to have his tires changed. He was impressed with the staff's attitude and their customer focus, and that made him feel more confident that the people there walk the company talk in how they manifest the values of the organization.

In the evaluation phase, you're often considering the interactions between multiple work-fit elements, but remember to examine each element independently as well.

Tips for Evaluating Each Work-Fit Element

Calculating the specifics of fit from outside the company when you're evaluating a potential employer is similar to evaluating a job from the inside, but there are significant differences, and it takes a lot more work! The questions are different and the specifics are harder to uncover because you have limited access to how the company really does things. You need to go through this process for every potential employer you want to evaluate.

Assess Your Potential Meaning Fit

Research

- Read what the company says about its mission and how it matters.

- Research articles, blogs, and media stories about the purpose of the organization and why it exists.

- Become familiar with its products or services.

- Mystery shop or visit the storefront to assess the customer experience.

- What does the company say in published material about what matters to them (values statement, mission, vision, annual report, employee handbook)?

(?) Ask

- Ask people you meet from the organization why they joined this company? Compare answers.
- Talk to current and past employees about the role that meaning plays in their jobs.
- Ask people who work there how they feel their job contributes to the mission of the organization.
- Ask people if they feel valued.
- Ask if managers have time for employees.

(👁) Observe

- Study the company's products and/or services closely, and ask people who work there why they're important.
- Notice how people informally talk about and connect to the organizational purpose.
- Look for evidence of meaning such as published values, inspiration, or company news.
- Do people seem to share themselves openly with others at work?
- Do people know each other's names and say hello in passing?

Calculate Your Potential Meaning Fit (Check all that apply)

- ☐ The things I care about also seem to matter to this company.
- ☐ I believe I'll be contributing to something important.
- ☐ I'm clear about what I'll be contributing.
- ☐ The job taps into my interests and passions.
- ☐ I would feel proud to be associated with this company.

How many items did you check for meaning fit? _____

Assess Your Potential Job Fit

○ Research

- List your key skills, experience, and interests and compare your list against the job description. Do the tasks and requirements line up well?

- Explore the types of jobs the company is filling and hiring patterns over time. Is your occupation well represented?

- Read glassdoor.com or indeed.com for information and reviews from people at the company who do a similar job.

(?) Ask

- Ask the prospective manager specific questions about:
  - Job responsibilities
  - Career path (including examples of people who have been hired for similar positions
  - Training opportunities
  - Performance feedback and the review process

- Interview individuals who are currently or have recently been in a similar job within the company about the work itself.

◉ Observe

- Are you genuinely excited about this job – not just about getting an offer?

- How are the people who are doing your job working day-to-day?

- Does the position seem to use people's talents and skills appropriately?

- Will the position help you advance your professional goals? If it won't, what are you getting out of it?

Calculate Your Potential Job Fit (Check all that apply)

☐ The job looks like a good match for my skills, interests, experience, training, and talents.

☐ I believe that I'll have opportunities at work to do what I really enjoy.

☐ I believe that I'll have the right resources and support to do my job.

☐ There appear to be opportunities to learn and grow in this job.

☐ There appears to be a clear expectation of what success looks like and clear processes for receiving feedback.

How many items did you check for job fit? _____

Assess Your Potential Culture Fit

🔍 Research

- Learn whatever you can online about the culture of the company, including mentions in social media, articles posted elsewhere, and especially to see what they say about themselves on their website.

- Read glassdoor.com or indeed.com for information and reviews from people at the company who do a similar job.

- Research best/great-places-to-work surveys in your industry and read what employees say.

💬 Ask

- Invite people you know who have worked in the company to meet and discuss their experiences. Ask them:
  - What was it like to work there?
  - How would you describe how the company does things?
  - Did you find that the company culture worked well for you? Why or why not?
  - How engaged did you feel with your job and with the company as a whole?

- During your job interview process ask everyone you meet how they would describe the company culture. Notice the words they use and how they feel to you.

- If you know individuals who are customers of the organization, ask them how they would describe the company culture.

Observe

- What do you notice about the "artifacts" of the company? The artifacts are the visible evidence of how the company does things, such as what messages are on the walls, what the physical space is like, what priorities are named in the employee handbook or recruitment material.

- How do people dress? Formal or informal? Outdoor ethnic or urban chic?

- How are offices set up? Open bullpen? Cubicles? Offices with doors? Common space?

- What feelings surface for you as you enter and experience the company? Does it feel like you? Does it make you uncomfortable?

Calculate Your Potential Culture Fit (Check all that apply)

- ☐ The organization's actions appear to match its values.
- ☐ Employees seem fully engaged.
- ☐ Employees seem vested in the company's success.
- ☐ I believe my communication style will work well there.
- ☐ I believe I will be able to be myself.

How many items did you check for culture fit? _____

Assess Your Potential Relationship Fit

Research

- Find former employees via LinkedIn and reach out to them about their experiences with their colleagues and their bosses.

- Do solid due diligence about your prospective boss by looking them up on social media and networking sites such as Facebook, LinkedIn, etc. Examine their career trajectory, their schooling, what other people say about them.

- Examine glassdoor.com and other employment websites to see what other employees say about working with managers and colleagues at this company.

- Looking at best/great-places-to-work surveys, notice the employee perspectives on trust.

⑦ Ask

- Ask people how they usually communicate with their coworkers (email, text, etc.).

- What are the organization's norms regarding conflict? Is it handled openly and directly? Is it invisible and/or suppressed? Does it seem acceptable to disagree with colleagues or with managers? Do you witness easy discussion about complex issues?

- What's the team structure in terms of day-to-day work? How often are formal or informal meetings scheduled?

- What's typically done to ensure team health?

- How do managers give and receive feedback?

◉ Observe

- Pay attention to the nuances of how your prospective boss seems in the interview (demeanor, body language, attire, office art).

- What's the energy level of prospective coworkers? Do they seem interested in your interview? In their jobs?

- How do people interact with the boss? Does it seem natural and easy? Formal? Efficient?

Calculate Your Potential Relationship Fit (Check all that apply)

☐ It appears that the manager and I share similar work-related values and philosophies.

☐ I've met people that I would enjoy spending time with.

☐ I see evidence that conflict is healthy and productive.

☐ Employees appear to trust and respect one another.

☐ I could see myself as part of this team.

How many items did you check for relationship fit? _____

Assess Your Potential Lifestyle Fit

Research

- Review best/great-places-to-work lists and see how the organization compares to others in the industry on lifestyle factors such as commute, work environment, and amenities.
- Read social media and LinkedIn posts from people you know who work there to see what comments they make about lifestyle.
- Does the company have any on-the-record statements about lifestyle and how it matters in how they do things? For example, is there a flextime policy? On-site childcare? Opportunity to volunteer for a nonprofit?
- Review the company's website for examples of working with employees in flexible ways.

Ask

- Ask about the organization's policies for:
  - Work from home
  - Flexible schedules
  - Onsite daycare
  - Concierge service for errands
  - Seasonal hours
  - Maternity/paternity leave
- Ask people you meet at the company about their lifestyle satisfaction.
- Ask your prospective boss what their lifestyle habits are vis-à-vis work. Do they work a lot of weekend hours? What's the expectation for cell phone availability?

Observe

- Observe the norms in addition to the policies. For example, the written policy on paternity leave may be 12 weeks, but how many people at your prospective level have taken it?
- How do people handle calls and email outside of working hours?
- Try doing the commute at rush hour. Can you see doing this routinely?

Calculate Your Potential Lifestyle Fit (Check all that apply)

- ☐ I believe that I'll be able to have the right balance between my job and time outside of work.

- ☐ I believe that I'll be able to meet my personal and family needs while also working productively.

- ☐ The job appears to be flexible in the ways I need it to be.

- ☐ Travel to and from work looks to be convenient.

- ☐ The company's written policies support my lifestyle needs.

How many items did you check for lifestyle fit? _____

Assess Your Potential Financial Fit

🔍 Research

- Know what your skills are worth. Use websites such as payscale.com or glassdoor.com to compare your prospective salary to those in similar jobs (factoring in things such as location, experience, and education).

- Calculate the total compensation package – salary, benefits, time off, perks such as gym membership, free food, and retirement.

- Know what compensation you need to make this job fit, which may be different from what you're making now.

⁇ Ask

- Make sure you ask questions about and fully understand all aspects of the offer:
  - What's included in your benefits package?
  - When does the health insurance coverage begin for new employees?
  - Does the company offer dental insurance? What's the plan?
  - Does the company offer vision insurance?
  - Does the company offer a discount on a gym membership or other perks?
  - What's the 401k – vesting, matching, can you roll over your current 401k into the new one?
  - Does the company offer life insurance or long-term disability insurance?

- How much paid vacation do they offer per year? Is it accrued over time? Does it carry over if you don't use all the days?
- How many sick and/or personal days do employees get?
- What are the official company paid holidays? If you have other religious holidays that fall outside of these, will the organization grant them?
- Do you get overtime for working over 40 hours?
- Do they offer a stock/equity package? What are the details and the vesting period?
- What's the bonus structure? Is it fixed based on personal goals or variable based on company performance?

• Ask for more than you need or want so that you can flex on the final offer.

• Take some time to think about the offer before responding.

◉〉 Observe

• When negotiating, prioritize and present what you need in rank order of importance (salary, vacation, benefits, location, bonus).

• Check out comments on social media or in the press about whether the pay at the company is perceived to be fair.

• Assess how the company is doing by reviewing its financial statements and other public information.

Calculate Your Potential Financial Fit (Click all that apply)

☐ I feel that the pay offered is fair.

☐ The overall structure of the compensation (fixed vs. variable, long- and short-term incentives, etc.) looks like it will meet my needs.

☐ There appears to be a good match between the demands of the job and the pay.

☐ There appears to be a good match between my needs and the benefits offered.

☐ I believe that I'll be able to take care of my responsibilities with what I'll be paid.

How many items did you check for financial fit? _____

ASSESSMENT OF YOUR POTENTIAL WORK FIT		
Fit Element	Rank of Importance	Number of Checkmarks You Selected
Meaning		
Job		
Culture		
Relationship		
Lifestyle		
Financial		

Figure 17-2. Rank the importance of each fit element from 1 (least important) to 6 (most important). Then enter the number of checkmarks you selected in assessing potential fit for each fit element. Were a lot of items checked for the most important elements of fit? If so, the organization you're assessing is likely to be a good fit for you.

Summary of Your Potential Work Fit Assessments

Congratulations on carefully considering the six elements of work fit as you explore a potential new employer. Let's look at your totals using the table in Figure 17-2.

Consider what work-fit elements are the most important to you right now. Were a lot of items checked for these important elements?

ASK YOURSELF . . .

- What have I learned from these assessments?
- What's the likelihood that this job will be a good work fit for me at this time?
- Are there areas where I've been overly optimistic?
- What are the risks if I'm wrong?

A 90-Day Research Project

Many employers have a 90-day probationary period during which an employee receives training, orientation, support, and feedback to ensure that they succeed on the job. If you decide, upon evaluation, to join a specific company and accept their offer, remember that it's not a forever arrangement. Consider the first 90 days on the job as a mutual research project. It's during this period that you and your new employer will get to know each other, and if there's potential for work misfit it will likely rear its ugly head within the first 90 days. If you see or feel something that's a red flag during this time, feel free to name it and work it out with your boss or team (see Chapter 15, "Flexing to Fit Where You Are"). And if the signs are extreme, at the end of the 90 days you can separate from the organization with less collateral damage than you (or they) would experience if you stayed longer.

With research revealing that many people will work for many organizations over the course of their lifetimes, it's important to learn how to assess fit early in your tenure and to move swiftly if you find yourself misfit. As David said, "In retrospect, it was the best thing that happened to me every time I left a bad fit for something else."

Pay Special Attention to Your Boss

Our research confirmed what's been widely touted in management archives, journals, blogs, and articles: the relationship with your direct supervisor is absolutely critical to the degree of happiness, satisfaction, and connection you feel at work. The voices of unfulfilled and frustrated employees ring in our heads.

- *I made the change to get away from an offensive manager.*
- *I had a boss who was abusive and it was demoralizing to be put down in front of others.*
- *A new boss didn't value my contributions and discouraged discussion/agreement.*

VERY IMPORTANT
It's critical that you get to know and spend time with your immediate boss when you evaluate new opportunities!

Make sure, before you accept a new opportunity, that you've spent time getting to know your potential new boss beyond a hasty interview.

Ask for time with them, and ask other people who work for them what they're like. If it's feasible, suggest an off-the-clock dinner or coffee, perhaps with spouses, to get to know the style and social dynamics of the person to whom you'll report. Notice how they behave under stress, how they treat salespeople, and what their office looks like. Imagine yourself getting direction from or delivering bad news to them. How easy is it to engage? Do they make eye contact? Seem interested in you? Listen attentively? People who meet with a prospective boss at least three times before accepting a job do much better in assessing whether the partnership will be a good one over time.

A Word About Intuition

Steve Jobs (2005) said in his now famous Stanford commencement speech, "Have the courage to follow your heart and intuition." But when it comes to assessing work fit, many people struggle to trust their own instincts. We tend to second-guess ourselves, especially if our confidence has been shaken by a misfit work experience.

Amidst a backdrop of self-doubt, when we're facing a change, it can be very difficult to pay attention to our instincts. These instincts evolve from our experience and wisdom formed over time. *Merriam-Webster* (2016) defines *intuition* as:

- A natural ability or power that makes it possible to know something without any proof or evidence: a feeling that guides a person to act a certain way without fully understanding why.

- Something that is known or understood without proof or evidence.

In order to assess a potential work situation, it's important that you complete the analysis, checklists, and spreadsheets we've reviewed so far. Don't shortchange this logical process and analysis. At the same time, it's essential to find ways to tap into your own instincts about the fit. To do this you must give yourself permission to spend time thinking and feeling about the potential organization. Pay attention to your intuition without deceiving yourself about an opportunity. We frequently overplay what looks good and underplay warning signs. But if we carefully examine what our gut is telling us (intuition), we'll be less likely to act hastily out of self-deception based on family, social, and internal pressures.

ASK YOURSELF ...

- What is my gut telling me about this?
- What makes my heart sing or delights me about this opportunity?
- How was my energy and flow after I met with people there?
- What am I telling others about the opportunity?
- Despite what other people say about this organization, can I picture myself there? Why or why not?

If you have trouble tapping into your gut instincts, try something new. For example, instead of list-making, sit quietly in a place you find relaxing and listen to your own thoughts. Listen to music, create art, or read or write poetry. Take a walk with a friend and talk about how you're feeling about the opportunity.

When you evaluate a new organization, take your time if you can, and understand what's at stake for you. When you find an organization that's right for you, you'll feel good. You'll feel energetic most of the time, look forward to going to work, tell others about your great company, and feel happy.

In the words of others who worked hard to find a great work fit, it's so worth the effort:

- *I had a great relationship with my manager, who is invested in my development. Finds my strengths valuable, and compensates me enough with a very reasonable work-life balance.* — Summer

- *I'm proud to represent my company, my founders, and their drive. I want to work hard for them and exceed expectations, and I hope to stay here for a length of time. I frankly could see myself here for life, I'm that happy. It's not perfect, but the things that are right for me, in sync with my style and values, are priceless to me.* — Robin

- *I was encouraged to do great work and utilize my strengths, challenged to stretch my knowledge and abilities, grow and learn. I always felt respected, but not always agreed with. Much laughter and authenticity among coworkers. Trust was built, valued, and maintained.* — Nancy

- *The term* in the flow *describes it well for me. Things are going well and normal daily obstacles feel solvable and manageable. I feel healthy and happy and productive both at work and at home.* — Deborah

- *It was great. I felt willing to go the extra mile and that my being there was valuable to them. What I brought to the table was of value. They truly cared about me and my work. I felt trusted. It seemed more like a family then a job.* — Richard

- *A sense of purpose, feeling valued, using the culmination of my past experiences and the ability to lead and coach others, allowing them growth opportunities in their own careers.* — Cheryl

Put on your sleuth hat, center yourself to evaluate options, and dig in to assess potential next companies. Follow your intuition, ask your trusted advisors, listen, and bravely jump when it feels right. Remember, there's no such thing as a perfect fit, so pay attention but don't obsess about the details too much. Your journey to finding great work fit is an unfolding story. The destination is elusive and transient, but so worth its noble pursuit.

The Future of Fit

Talented people need organizations less than organizations need talented people.

— Dan Pink

W E CAN SEE IT CLEAR AS DAY . . .

Happy people of all cultures and walks of life joyously working every day. Their spirits are light and you can feel the contentment radiating off them. Their productivity is high and they deeply believe that what they're doing every day is important and matters to someone, no matter what job or position they hold. Beyond fitting in at work, these people feel well suited both to their exact job, and to the organization that they have joined, at least for now. People's lives are working. Men and women equally, across race and other identity aspects, feel energized and motivated to do a great job. While every day is not bliss, on the whole, over time, people are thriving in their places of work, and thus organizations are meeting their mission and profit goals, the global economy is succeeding, and families and communities are healthier.

Ahhhhhh.

Feels good, right?

Can we get there? What will it really take?

203

We believe that the first step is for people, employees at work, to take charge of their own love affair with their jobs. All social change movements start when a small group of people claim a point of view and actively work together to make change happen. Acknowledge the importance of work fit to you, your well-being, the well-being of your family, your community, your organization, and the world at large. Consider what it would mean to actively pursue great fit as a central component of your health.

Follow the tips in this book to find great work fit for yourself as soon as you can.

Know that great work fit is temporally fleeting, so don't give up if you find yourself misfit over time. And if, after reading this book, you're able to improve your work fit, or, even better, secure a job that you love (for now), we'll know that the book will have been worth writing.

Our Dream

Our fundamental dream, however, goes way beyond each of you activating an individual change. In our image of the future of work fit, organizations actively design themselves to be great places for human beings to work, now and tomorrow. Leaders, from the CEO to the frontline managers, choose to pay attention to fit and create workplaces in which the people who work for them thrive. These leaders consider the six elements of work fit in how they configure their offices, in how they compensate people, in how they train and invest in people, in how they help people live full and healthy lives, in how they make work meaningful, in how they partner at work, and in how they can build a company culture where people grow.

Work fit becomes part of the conversation for organizations large and small, right up there with profit margin, shareholder equity, and waste metrics. Leaders look at their ability to be good for the people who work for them as a measure of their results, not as an afterthought once the numbers are in.

When this happens, the unimaginable takes place.

Each and every employee, whether frontline or executive, gets a little more connected, to themselves, to the work, and to each other. In that connective spirit they're inspired to work hard, to bring their best effort forward, which cascades into a cycle of excellence. There is more joy, more love, more grace, and more cooperation than ever before. Customers feel the impact and want more.

People loving their jobs can and will change the world. We believe it. And we invite all leaders out there to act as if they believe it, too.

Let's get on it.

Analyze Your Employability Skills

THE FOLLOWING EXERCISE provides helpful prompts for identifying your current skills and areas where you would like more development. The eight skills listed are frequently sought by employers and aren't exclusively related to any single career. Remember that this is an initial self-assessment exercise to help you to determine which skills are of importance to you in planning your future. Few people are likely to have developed the majority of these skills to a high level. *Don't feel that a low rating in any skill area is an admission of failure* – you may have no wish to use that skill or you may be able to improve upon it with a little practice.

ANALYZING YOUR EMPLOYABILITY SKILLS		
Go through the following list of skills, selecting any that you feel you already have or would like to develop. Ignore those that you don't feel are relevant to you.		
WRITTEN COMMUNICATION	I Have This	I'd Like to Improve This
Thinking through in advance what you want to say		
Report writing skills		
Gathering, analyzing, and arranging data in a logical sequence		

Developing your argument in a logical way		
Briefly summarizing the content		
Adapting your writing style for different audiences		
Avoiding jargon		

VERBAL COMMUNICATION	I Have This	I'd Like to Improve This
Accurately hearing what others are saying		
Able to clarify and summarize what others are communicating		
Being sensitive to others' values and feelings		
Not interrupting		
Helping others to define their problems		
Telephone skills (thinking through in advance what you want to say; keeping business calls to the point)		
Making a speech in front of an audience (thinking up an interesting way to put across your message, structuring your presentation, using audio-visual aids effectively, successfully building a rapport with your audience)		
Making effective use of body language, dress, conduct, speech		

INVESTIGATING AND ANALYZING	I Have This	I'd Like to Improve This
Clarifying the nature of a problem before deciding action		
Collecting, collating, classifying, and summarizing data		
Being able to use results effectively using text/graphs/tables/pictures		
Finding where the required information is available		
Gathering information systematically		

Formulating questions		
Being able to condense information/produce summary notes		
PLANNING AND ORGANIZING	I Have This	I'd Like to Improve This
Managing your time effectively using action planning skills		
Prioritizing tasks effectively		
Setting objectives that are achievable and measurable		
Identifying the steps needed to achieve goals		
Using lists		
Being able to work effectively under pressure/managing stress		
Completing work to make a deadline		
NEGOTIATING AND PERSUADING	I Have This	I'd Like to Improve This
Developing a line of reasoned argument		
Emphasizing the positive aspects of your argument		
Understanding the needs of who you're dealing with		
Using tact and diplomacy		
Handling objections to your arguments		
Making concessions to reach agreement		
Challenging the points of view expressed by others		
COOPERATING (GROUPWORK)	I Have This	I'd Like to Improve This
Contributing your own ideas effectively in a group		

	I Have This	I'd Like to Improve This
Taking a share of the responsibility in a group		
Being assertive – rather than passive or aggressive		
Accepting and learning from constructive criticism and giving positive, constructive feedback to others		
Concentrating on behavior that can be improved		
Identifying your strengths and weaknesses		
LEADERSHIP	**I Have This**	**I'd Like to Improve This**
Setting objectives		
Organizing and motivating others		
Taking the initiative		
Persevering when things are not working out		
Taking a positive attitude to frustration/failure		
Accepting responsibility for mistakes/wrong decisions		
Being flexible – prepared to adapt goals in the light of changing situations		
NUMERACY Being able to do the following:	**I Have This**	**I'd Like to Improve This**
Use simple statistics		
Calculate percentages		
Multiply and divide accurately		
Read and interpret graphs and tables		
Use a calculator		
Manage a limited budget		
Managing a budget		

Holland's Six Occupation Types

Type	Description	Example Occupations
Realistic	Interest in activities requiring motor coordination, motor skill, and physical strength. People oriented toward the Realistic type prefer acting out problems or being physically involved in performing work tasks: they typically avoid tasks involving interpersonal and verbal skills and seek concrete rather than abstract problem situations.	Mechanic, Electrician, Farmer, Engineer
Investigative	Main characteristics include thinking rather than acting, organizing and understanding rather than dominating or persuading, and associability rather than sociability. Investigative types prefer to avoid close, interpersonal contact, though the quality of their avoidance seems different from that of their Realistic colleagues.	Biologist, Chemist, Physicist, Researcher

Artistic	Manifestations of strong self-expression and relations with people through artistic expression are central to Artistic types. They tend to dislike structure and prefer tasks emphasizing physical skills or interpersonal interactions. They tend to be introspective and social much in the manner of the Investigative, but they often express emotion more readily than most people.	Writer, Designer, Musician, Actor
Social	Social types generally gravitate to activities that involve promoting the health, education, or well-being of others. Unlike Realistic and Investigative types, Social types tend to seek close relationships. They are apt to be socially skilled and often averse to isolative activities, as well as to activities that require extensive physical functioning or intellectual problem solving.	Teacher, Social worker, Minister, Psychologist
Enterprising	Although often verbally skilled, Enterprising types tend to use these skills for self-gain rather than to support others, as do Social types. They frequently are concerned about power and status, as are Conventional types, but differ in that they usually aspire to attain power and status, while the Conventional types honor others for it.	Manager, Buyer, Salesperson, Executive
Conventional	Typified by great concern for rules and regulations, great self-control, subordination of personal needs and strong identification with power and status. Conventional types prefer structure and order and thus seek interpersonal and work situations where structure abounds.	Accountant, Banker, Analyst, Bookkeeper

Source: "Holland's Theory of Vocational Choice." Career Research
http://career.iresearchnet.com/career-development/hollands-theory-of-vocational-choice/

Assessment Tool Comparison Chart

Assessment Tool	Description
Gallup Strengthsfinder: 5 Dominant Themes – Book Version	Self report. Discover natural talents/strengths (as opposed to skills and knowledge). Based on positive psychology model. Other 29 themes not included.
Firo B	Behaviors relating to inclusion, control and affection; insights essential for relationships and team engagement. Used well with MBTI.
5 Dynamics	Energy management + styles: How individuals learn, work, and collaborate; great tool for addressing "fit" between a person's strengths and their jobs and roles.
Myers-Briggs	Provides effective measure of personality type by looking at eight preferences organized into four dichotomies. The four preferences (one from each scale) are combined into one's personality type. There are 16 personality types. Can also use temperament theory based on Kiersey's temperament model.
Thomas Killman Conflict Mode	Based on a continuum of cooperativeness and assertiveness. Measures the five conflict handling modes: collaborating, competing, accomodating, compromising, and avoiding.

Strong Interest Inventory	Assessment provides framework for matching interests with opportunities for jobs/education. Based on Holland's theory.
Everything DiSC	Measures observable behavior. Assessment of style along two dimensions, producing a unique graph of each person's style profile. Four styles: dominance, influence, steadiness, and compliance.
Change Style Indicator	Comprehensive report based on 4–5 key leadership competencies and related management skills. Assesses a leader's strengths and weaknesses from executives to managers to individual contributors.
Emotional Intelligence Appraisal – Me Edition	Measures overall emotional quotient (EQ), self-awareness, self-management, social awareness, and relationship management. Results bring EQ to life in an unlimited e-learning program featuring proprietary Goal-Tracking System, EQ lessons, and retest.
Enneagram	The Riso-Hudson Enneagram Type Indicator (RHETI version 2.5), identifies basic personality types. The Enneagram uses numbers to designate each of the types because numbers are value neutral – they imply the whole range of attitudes and behaviors of each type without specifying anything either positive or negative.

Work Relationships Matrix

Person's Name	Importance to You	Frequency of Interactions	Trust Level (1–10)	Ease of Interactions

Is It Time to Leave? Assessment

Check all of the statements below that apply to you.
☐ I do not look foward to going to work most days.
☐ I am asked to do things that are unethical and/or violate my values.
☐ I received a subpar performance review.
☐ My job regularly interferes with my work-life balance.
☐ I do not get along with my boss.
☐ I regularly consider leaving my job.
☐ I do not have professional development opportunities in my position.
☐ If I were offered a solid position right now, even if it paid less, I would consider it.
☐ There is no growth potential for me in my company.
☐ I am overqualified for my position.
☐ I have difficulty working with most of my colleagues.

- ☐ I had a recent disagreement with my boss or peer.

- ☐ I complain regularly about my workplace to my family and friends.

- ☐ I am checking job postings more often as time goes on.

- ☐ My appearance and health habits have changed for the worse.

- ☐ People are leaving my team and/or company for better opportunities at other companies.

- ☐ I have taken a sick day here and there because I dread going to work.

- ☐ My daily tasks are repetitive.

- ☐ I feel that I could find a better compensation package elsewhere.

- ☐ I am unhappy with my work commute.

SCORING

If you checked 1–3 statements: You are probably more satisfied than not on a given day. See what you can do to address any issues you may be experiencing.

If you checked 4–8 statements: Consider talking to your boss, a colleague you trust, or HR to see if there's anything you can do to address the areas that you're unhappy with.

If you checked 8–13 statements: You're pretty unhappy with your job. Consider whether or not the areas that you're unhappy with can be enhanced. This may not happen fast enough or meet your standards. Perhaps consider looking for other opportunities while you're assessing whether or not change can happen.

If you checked 14 or more statements: You should probably consider leaving. Indeed, there may be room for some change, but in your case, there would need to be a lot of change and fast! Of course, you may want to look for another opportunity while you're still employed, since it's often easier to find a new job while you still have one.

Research developed by Amy Wrzesniewski.

Culture Fit Questions to Ask

Below are questions to ask various people to help you assess organizational culture fit.

Ask Your Potential Boss

- I'd love to know how you think about your role as leader or manager . . . what matters to you about that job?
- How has your career led to this role?
- In what ways does this company invest in your learning to lead?
- Describe a time when you hired someone who was the wrong culture fit. Why do you think it happened and what was the result?
- What kind of people do you think do really well here?

Ask a Potential Coworker

- What do you love about this company?
- What sometimes makes it tiring/hard/disappointing to work here?
- Tell me about the team you work with. How do they like to work?
- In what ways does the team interact and communicate and how does that work for you?
- Is trust a currency that's visible here? How so or not?

Ask a Past Employee

- What did your time working with the company mean for you?
- What specifics led to you finding a better fit?
- What three words would you use to describe the culture there?
- Are there any red flags you think I should examine closely?

Ask a Current Employee

- Why did you choose this company?
- Where do you see yourself within the company in the next three years?
- What have you learned here?
- Who do you most admire?

Ask a Senior Leader

- How do you experience the culture here?
- How does culture get talked about at the top of the company? At other levels?
- In what ways does the internal culture here match the demands of the external environment?
- What do you think is leadership's role in stewarding culture?
- If you were me, what would you be thinking about in terms of culture fit?

Ask a Vendor

- What's it like to be a supplier to the company?
- What's the vibe of your interactions in terms of how they do business, pay bills, follow up, solve problems, give feedback, etc.?
- In what ways are they an ideal customer for you, or not?

Ask a Customer

- Why have you chosen to purchase services or goods from the company?
- How would you describe the staff you interact with regularly?
- Based on your interactions so far, how would you describe the company culture?

BIBLIOGRAPHY

ADAA. 2006. "Highlights: Workplace Stress & Anxiety Disorders Survey." Anxiety and Depression Association of America. https://www.adaa.org/workplace-stress-anxiety-disorders-survey.

Adkins, Amy. 2015. "Majority of U.S. Employees Not Engaged Despite Gains in 2014." Gallup Poll, January 28. http://www.gallup.com/poll/181289/majority-employees-not-engaged-despite-gains-2014.aspx.

———. 2016. "Employee Engagement in U.S. Stagnant in 2015." Gallup Poll, January 13. http://www.gallup.com/poll/188144/employee-engagement-stagnant-2015.aspx.

Aon Hewitt. 2015. *2015 Trends in Global Human Engagement.* London: Aon.

Ariga, Astunori, and Alejandro Lleras. 2011. "Brief and Rare Mental 'Breaks' Keep You Focused: Deactivation and Reactivation of Task Goals Preempt Vigilance Decrements." *Cognition.* doi: 10.1016/j.cognition.2010.12.007.

Artz, Benjamin, A. Goodall, and A. Oswald. 2016. "Boss Competence and Worker Well Being." *ILR Review,* May 16.

Babcock, Linda, and Sara Laschever. 2007. *Women Don't Ask: The High Cost of Avoiding Negotiation – and Positive Strategies for Change.* Reprint edition. New York: Bantam Books.

Baikei, Karen A., and Kay Wilhelm. 2005. "Emotional and Physical Health Benefits of Expressive Writing." *Advances in Psychiatric Treatment* 11 (5):338–346. doi: 10.1192/apt.11.5.338.

Bates, Steve. 2004. "Getting Engaged." *HR Magazine,* February 1. https://www.shrm.org/hr-today/news/hr-magazine/pages/0204covstory.aspx.

Baumeister, Roy F., Kathleen D. Vohs, Jennifer L. Aaker, and Emily N. Garbinsky. 2013. "Some Key Differences between a Happy Life and a Meaningful Life." *The Journal of Positive Psychology,* Vol. 8, Iss. 6,2013.

Benson, Herbert, and Miriam Z. Klipper. 2000. *The Relaxation Response,* reissue edition. New York: HarperTorch.

Bersin, Josh, Dimple Agarwal, Bill Pelster, and Jeff Schwartz. 2015. *Global Human Capital Trends.* New York: Deloitte University Press.

Bersin, Josh. 2013. "Employee Retention Now a Big Issue: Why the Tide Has Turned." Bersin by Deloitte, August 16. https://www.linkedin.com/pulse/20130816200159-131079-employee-retention-now-a-big-issue-why-the-tide-has-turned.

———. 2015. "Predictions for 2015: Redesigning the Organization for a Rapidly Changing World." Bersin by Deloitte, January 6. http://blog.bersin.com/predictions-for-2015-redesigning-the-organization-for-a-rapidly-changing-world/.

Block, Peter. 2009. *Community: The Structure of Belonging*. San Francisco: Berrett-Koehler.

Boehm, J. K., and S. Lyubomirsky. 2008. "Does Happiness Promote Career Success?" *Journal of Career Assessment* 16 (1):101–116. doi: 10.1177/1069072707308140.

Borysenko, Karlyn. 2015. "What Was Management Thinking? The High Cost of Employee Turnover." TLNT: Talent Management and HR, April 22. https://www.eremedia.com/tlnt/what-was-leadership-thinking-the-shockingly-high-cost-of-employee-turnover/.

Boushey, Heather, and Bridget Ansel. 2016. *Overworked America: The Economic Causes and Consequences of Long Work Hours*. Washington, DC: Washington Center for Equitable Growth.

Boushey, Heather, and Sarah Jane Glynn. 2012. *There Are Significant Business Costs to Replacing Employees*. Washington, DC: Center for American Progress.

Brown, Brené. 2010. *The Gifts of Imperfection: Let Go of Who You Think You're Supposed to Be and Embrace Who You Are*. Center City, MN: Hazelden.

———. 2015. *Daring Greatly: How the Courage to be Vulnerable Transforms the Way We Live, Love, Parent, and Lead*. New York: Avery Publishing.

———. 2015. *Rising Strong*. New York: Spiegel & Grau.

Bulygo, Zach. 2015. "Building a Strong Company Culture with AirBnB CEO Brian Chesky." Kissmetrics. https://blog.kissmetrics.com/brian-chesky-alfred-lin-culture/.

Bureau of Labor Statistics. 2014. "Charts from the American Time Use Survey." U.S. Department of Labor. http://www.bls.gov/tus/charts/home.htm.

———. 2015. "Number of Jobs Held, Labor Market Activity, and Earnings Growth Among the Youngest Baby Boomers: Results From a Longitudinal Survey." U.S. Department of Labor, March 21.

Cameron, Julia. 2002. *The Artist's Way*. New York: Jeremy P. Tarcher/Putnam.

Campbell, Angus, Phillip E. Converse, and Willard L. Rodgers. 1976. *The Quality of American Life, Perceptions, Evaluations, and Satisfactions*. New York: Russell Sage Foundation.

Chatman, Jennifer A. 1991. "Managing People and Organizations: Selection and Socialization in Public Accounting Firms." *Administrative Science Quarterly* 36:459–484.

Choney, Suzanne. 2016. "The Changing World of Work." Microsoft and Pop Tech video. https://www.youtube.com/watch?v=95o-jz50AaQ.

Circadian. 2005. *Absenteeism: The Bottom-Line Killer*. Lexington, MA: Circadian Information Limited Partnership.

Coelho, Paulo. 1994. *The Alchemist*, translated by Alan R. Clarke. San Francisco: HarperSanFrancisco.

Coleman, John, Daniel Gulati, Bill George, and W. Oliver Segovia. 2012. *Passion and Purpose: Stories from the Best and Brightest Young Business Leaders*. Boston: Harvard Business Review Press.

Colten, Harvey R., and Bruce M. Altevogt, eds. 2006. "Extent and Health Consequences of Chronic Sleep Loss and Sleep Disorders." In *Sleep Disorders and Sleep Deprivation: An Unmet Public Health Problem*. Washington, DC: The National Academies Press.

Covey, Stephen R. 1989. *The 7 Habits of Highly Effective People: Restoring the Character Ethic*. New York: Free Press.

Craig, Nick, and Scott A. Snook. 2014. "From Purpose to Impact." *Harvard Business Review*, May. https://hbr.org/2014/05/from-purpose-to-impact.

Cropanzano, Russell, and Thomas A Wright. 1999. "A 5-Year Study of Change in the Relationship between Well-Being and Job Performance." *Consulting Psychology Journal: Practice and Research* 51 (4):252.

Crowell, Beverly, Lynn Coward, and Beverly Kaye. 2013. "Engagement Leads to Growth at Morrison." *Talent Management*, July.

Cubiks 2013. *International Survey on Job and Cultural Fit*. Guildford, Surrey: Cubiks.

Deloitte. 2016. *The 2016 Deloitte Millennial Survey: Winning Over the Next Generation of Leaders*. London: Deloitte Touche Tohmatsu Limited.

Denison, Daniel R. 1990. *Corporate Culture and Organizational Effectiveness, Wiley Series on Organizational Assessment and Change*. Oxford, England: John Wiley & Sons.

Denison. 2010. *Research Notes: Organizational Culture & Employee Engagement: What's the Relationship?* Volume 4, Issue 3. Denison Consulting. https://www.denisonconsulting.com/sites/default/files/documents/resources/rn_engagement_0.pdf.

———. 2013. *Research Notes: What Are You Really Measuring with a Culture Survey?* Volume 8, Issue 1. Denison Consulting. https://www.denisonconsulting.com/sites/default/files/documents/resources/culture_effectiveness.pdf.

Doward, Jamie. 2010. "Happy People Really Do Work Harder." *The Guardian*, July 10. https://www.theguardian.com/science/2010/jul/11/happy-workers-are-more-productive.

Dweck, Carol. 2007. *Mindset: The New Psychology of Success*. New York: Ballantine Books.

Flade, Peter, Jim Harter, Jim Asplund. 2014. "Seven Things Great Employers Do (That Others Don't)." *Gallup Business Journal,* April 15. http://www.gallup. com/businessjournal/168407/seven-things-great-employers-others-don. aspx.

Fox, Killian, and Joanne O'Connor. 2015. "Five Ways Work Will Change in the Future." *The Guardian,* November 29. https://www.theguardian.com/ society/2015/nov/29/five-ways-work-will-change-future-of-workplace-ai-cloud-retirement-remote.

Frankl, Viktor E. 1959. *Man's Search for Meaning.* Translated by Ilse Lasch. Boston: Beacon Press. Originally published in 1946 as *trotzdem Ja zum Leben sagen.*

Fry, Richard. 2016. "Millennials Overtake Baby Boomers as America's Largest Generation." Pew Research Center, April 25. http://www.pewresearch.org/ fact-tank/2016/04/25/millennials-overtake-baby-boomers/.

Galinsky, Ellen, Kerstin Aumann, and James T. Bond. 2009. "Times Are Changing: Gender and Generation at Work and at Home." *National Study of the Changing Workforce 2008.* New York: Families and Work Institute.

Gallup. 2013. *State of the American Workplace: Employee Engagement Insights for U.S. Business Leaders.* Washington, DC: Gallup. http://www.gallup.com/ services/176708/state-american-workplace.aspx.

Garton, Eric, Michael C. Mankins. 2015. "Engaging Your Employees Is Good, but Don't Stop There." *Harvard Business Review,* December. https://hbr. org/2015/12/engaging-your-employees-is-good-but-dont-stop-there.

Gates, Stephen. 2003. *Linking People Measures to Strategy.* Ottawa: The Conference Board of Canada.

George, J.M. 1991. "State or Trait: Effects of Positive Mood on Prosocial Behaviors at Work." *Journal of Applied Psychology* 76:299–307.

Gillespie, Michael A., Daniel R. Denison, Stephanie Haaland, Ryan Smerek, and William S. Neale. 2007. "Linking Organizational Culture and Customer Satisfaction: Results from Two Companies." *European Journal of Work and Organizational Psychology.* doi: 10.1080/13594320701560820.

Gladding, Rebecca. 2011. "Don't Believe Everything You Think or Feel." *Psychology Today,* June. https://www.psychologytoday.com/blog/use-your-mind-change-your-brain/201106/don-t-believe-everything-you-think-or-feel.

Gladwell, Malcom. 2002. *The Tipping Point: How Little Things Can Make a Big Difference.* New York: Back Bay Books.

Gourlay, Alex. 2009. *Healthy People = Healthy Profits.* London: Business in the Community.

Gouveia, Aaron. 2013. "Salary Neotiation: Separating Fact from Fiction." Salary. com, September 22. http://www.salary.com/salary-negotiation-separating-fact-from-fiction/.

Gray, Jeremy R. 1999. "A Bias Toward Short-Term Thinking in Threat-Related Negative Emotional States." *Personality and Social Pychology Bulletin* 25 (1):65–75. doi: 10.1177/0146167299025001006

Headspace. 2013. "Meditation in Action: 5 Tips for Incorporating Mindfulness into a Tech-Centric World." *The Huffington Post*, June 3. http://www.huffingtonpost.com/2013/06/03/meditation-in-action-technology-and-mindfulness_n_3360037.html.

Heffernan, Margaret. 2015a. *Beyond Measure: The Big Impact of Small Changes.* New York: Simon & Schuster/TED Books.

———. 2015b. "The Secret Ingredient that Makes Some Teams Better than Others." TED, May 5. http://ideas.ted.com/the-secret-ingredient-that-makes-some-teams-better-than-others/.

Heilman, Brian, Geneva Cole, Kenneth Matos, Alexa Hassink, Ron Mincy, and Gary Barker. 2016. *State of America's Fathers.* Washington, DC: MenCare Advocacy.

Hennessey, Ray. 2016. "Good Company Culture is Not About Silly, Attention Grabbing Perks." *Entrepreneur*, June 25. https://www.entrepreneur.com/article/276679.

Heshmat, Shahram. 2015. "What Is Confirmation Bias?" *Psychology Today*, April 23. https://www.psychologytoday.com/blog/science-choice/201504/what-is-confirmation-bias.

Hilbrecht, Margo, Bryan Smale, and Steven E. Mock. 2014. "Highway to Health? Commute Time and Well-being among Canadian Adults." *World Leisure Journal* 56 (2):151–163. doi: 10.1080/16078055.2014.903723.

Holland, John L. 1997. *Making Vocational Choices: A Theory of Vocational Personalities and Work Environnments,* Third Edition. Odessa, FL: Psychological Assessment Resources.

Iverson, Roderick D, Mara Olekalns, and Peter J Erwin. 1998. "Affectivity, Organizational Stressors, and Absenteeism: A Causal Model of Burnout and Its Consequences." *Journal of Vocational Behavior* 52 (1):1–23.

Jaffe, Eric. 2014. "Science Confirms It: Your Crappy Boss Is Making You Unhappy." *Fast Company*, November 12. https://www.fastcodesign.com/3038394/evidence/science-confirms-it-your-crappy-boss-is-making-you-unhappy?

Jernigan, I.E., III, Joyce M. Beggs, and Gary F. Kohut. 2002. "Dimensions of Work Satisfaction as Predictors of Commitment Type." *Journal of Managerial Psychology* 17 (7):564–579. doi:10.1108/02683940210444030.

Jobs, Steve. 2005. "You've Got to Find What You Love." Stanford University Commencement Address. *Stanford News,* June 12. http://news.stanford.edu/2005/06/14/jobs-061505/.

Johnson, Shana Montesol, and Brendan Rigby. 2012. *Peer Coaching Guidelines.* Melbourne, Australia: WhyDev.

Kahneman, D., and A. Deaton. 2010. "High Income Improves Evaluation of Life but Not Emotional Well-being." *Proceedings of the National Academy of Sciences of the United States of America* 107 (38):16489–93. doi: 10.1073/pnas.1011492107.

Kan, Michelle, Gad Levanon, Allen Li, and Rebecca L. Ray. 2016. *Job Satisfaction: 2016 Edition.* New York: The Conference Board.

Kantor, Jodi, and David Streitfeld. 2015. "Inside Amazon: Wrestling Big Ideas in a Bruising Workplace." *New York Times*, August 16. http://www.nytimes.com/2015/08/16/technology/inside-amazon-wrestling-big-ideas-in-a-bruising-workplace.html?_r=1.

Katz, Lawrence F., and Alan B. Krueger. 2016. "The Rise and Nature of Alternative Work Arrangements in the United States, 1995–2015." NBER Working Paper No. 22667, September. National Bureau of Economic Research.

Kauffman, Carol, and Diane Coutu. 2008. *HBR Research Report: The Realities of Executive Coaching.* Brighton, MA: Harvard Business School Publishing.

Kelleher, Bob. 2010. "Louder Than Words." In *Ten Practical Employee Engagement Steps that Drive Results*, edited by Liz Batchelder. Portland, OR: BLKB Publishing.

Kobau, Rosemarie, Joseph Sniezek, Mathew M. Zack, Richard E. Lucas, and Adam Burns. 2010. "Well-Being Assessment: An Evaluation of Well-Being Scales for Public Health and Population Estimates of Well-Being among US Adults." *Applied Psychology: Health and Well-Being* 2 (4):272–297. doi: 10.1111/j.1758-0854.2010.01035.x.

Kouzes, James, and Barry Z. Posner. 2012. *The Leadership Challenge.* Fifth Edition. San Fransisco: Jossy-Bass.

Kowalsky, Diana. 2012. "Around the Company Campfire." CFM, August 23. http://www.cfm-online.com/marketing-pr-blog/2012/8/23/around-the-company-campfire.html.

Lee, Duck-chul, Russell R. Pate, Carl J. Lavie, Xuemei Sui, Timothy S. Church, and Steven N. Blair. 2014. "Leisure-Time Running Reduces All-Cause and Cardiovascular Mortality Risk." *Journal of the American College of Cariology* 64 (5):472–481. doi: 10.1016/j.jacc.2014.04058.

Lee, Thomas W., and Terence R. Mitchell. 1991. "The Unfolding Effects of Organizational Commitment and Anticipated Job Satisfaction on Voluntary Employee Turnover." *Motivation and Emotion* 15 (1):99-121. doi: 10.1007/bf00991478.

Lencioni, Patrick M. 2003. "Drucker Foundation's Leader to Leader, No. 29 – The Trouble with Teamwork." The Table Group, June. http://www.table-group.com/blog/drucker-foundations-leader-to-leader-no-29-the-trouble-with-teamwork.

———. 2015. *The Truth About Employee Engagement: A Fable About Addressing the Three Root Causes of Job Misery*. San Francisco: Jossey-Bass.

———. 2016. *The Ideal Team Player: How to Recognize and Cultivate the Three Essential Virtues*. San Francisco: Jossey-Bass.

Lencioni, Patrick. 2002. *The Five Dysfunctions of a Team: A Leadership Fable*. San Francisco: Jossey-Bass.

Lipman, Victor. 2014. "Want Motivated Employees? Offer Ample Opportunities For Growth." *Forbes Magazine*, January 24.

———. 2015. *The Type B Manager: Leading Successfully in a Type A World*. New York: Prentice Hall Press.

Lok, Peter, and John Crawford. 1999. "The Relationship Between Commitment and Organizational Culture, Subculture, Leadership Style and Job Satisfaction in Organizational Change and Development." *Leadership & Organization Development Journal* 20 (7):365–374. doi: doi:10.1108/01437739910302524.

Mann, Annamarie, and Becky McCarville. 2015. "What Job-Hopping Employees Are Looking For." *Gallup Business Journal,* November 13. http://www.gallup.com/businessjournal/186602/job-hopping-employees-looking.aspx.

Marciano, Paul. 2010. *Carrots and Sticks Don't Work*. New York: McGraw-Hill.

Margulies, Newton, and Anthony P. Raia. 1972. *Organizational Development: Values, Process, and Technology*. New York: McGraw-Hill.

Maslow, A. H. 1943. "A Theory of Human Motivation." *Psychology Review* 50:370–396.

Maylett, Tracy, and Paul Warner. 2014. *MAGIC: Five Keys to Unlock the Power of Employee Engagement*. Austin, TX: Greenleaf Book Group Press.

Meister, Jeanne. 2012. "Job Hopping is the 'New Normal' for Millennials: Three Ways to Prevent a Human Resource Nightmare." *Forbes,* August 14. http://www.forbes.com/sites/jeannemeister/2012/08/14/job-hopping-is-the-new-normal-for-millennials-three-ways-to-prevent-a-human-resource-nightmare/ - 204fc5645508.

Merriam-Webster. 2014. "Merriam-Webster Announces 'Culture' as 2014 Word of the Year." *Merriam-Webster,* December 15. http://www.merriam-webster.com/press-release/2014-word-of-the-year.

———. 2016. "Intuition." *Merriam-Webster.com.* http://www.merriam-webster.com/dictionary/intuition.

Morgan, Jacob. 2014a. "7 Principles of the Future Employee." The Future Organization, November 10. https://thefutureorganization.com/7-seven-principles-future-employee/.

———. 2014b. "The Top 10 Factors for On-the-Job Employee Happiness." *Forbes,* December 15. http://www.forbes.com/sites/jacobmorgan/2014/12/15/the-top-10-factors-for-on-the-job-employee-happiness/#217227a744fe.

Neff, Kristen. 2015. *Self-Compassion: The Proven Power of Being Kind to Yourself.* Reprint edition. New York: William Morrow Paperbacks.

Nunberg, Geoff. 2016. "Goodbye Jobs, Hello 'Gigs': How One Word Sums Up a New Economic Reality." National Public Radio, January 11. http://www. npr.org/2016/01/11/460698077/goodbye-jobs-hello-gigs-nunbergs-word-of-the-year-sums-up-a-new-economic-reality.

Nuñez, Mario. 2015. "Does Money Buy Happiness? The Link Between Salary and Employee Satisfaction." Glassdoor, June 18. https://www.glassdoor. com/research/does-money-buy-happiness-the-link-between-salary-and-employee-satisfaction/.

O.C. Tanner. n.d. "Social Capital Is Key to Better Team Engagement." Emergenetics International. https://www.emergenetics.com/blog/social-capital-team-engagement/.

Oswald, Andrew J., Eugenio Proto, and Daniel Sgroi. 2014. *Happiness and Productivity.* Coventry, UK: University of Warwick. https://www2.warwick.ac.uk/ fac/soc/economics/staff/eproto/workingpapers/happinessproductivity.pdf.

Ouye, Joe Aki. 2011. *Five Trends that Are Dramatically Changing Work and the Workplace.* East Greenville, PA: Knoll.

Pan, Joanna. 2012. "Smartphones Extend Our Workdays by Two Hours." *Mashable,* October 31. http://mashable.com/2012/10/31/smartphones-work-study/#_hp6.jvhgkqr.

Parker, Kim, and Wendy Wang. 2013a. "Chapter 5: Americans' Time at Paid Work, Housework, Child Care, 1965 to 2011." In *Modern Parenthood: Roles of Moms and Dads Converge as They Balance Work and Family.* Washington, DC: Pew Research Center.

———. 2013b. *Modern Parenthood: Roles of Moms and Dads Converge as They Balance Work and Family.* Washington, DC: Pew Research Center.

Parker-Pope, Tara. 2010. "An Ugly Toll of Technology: Impatience and Forgetfulness." *The New York Times,* June 6.

Paton, Cassie. 2015. "37 Company Culture Quotes that Will Inspire Your Team." Enplug, August 25. https://enplug.com/blog/37-company-culture-quotes-that-will-inspire-your-team

Patterson, Kerry, Joseph Grenny, Ron McMillan, and Al Switzler. 2011. *Crucial Conversations,* Updated Second Edition. New York: McGraw-Hill Education.

PayScale. 2015. "Inside the Gender Pay Gap." PayScale. http://www.payscale. com/data-packages/gender-pay-gap.

Pencavel, John. 2014. *The Productivity of Working Hours.* Bonn, Germany: Institute for the Study of Labor (IZA).

Pink, Daniel H. 2009. *"Harvard Business Review* On What Really Motivates Workers." http://www.danpink.com/2009/12/harvard-business-review-on-what-really-motives-workers/.

Pink, Daniel H. 2011. *Drive: The Surprising Truth About What Motivates Us.* New York: Riverhead Books.

Posner, B. Z. 2010. "Values and the American Manager: A Three-Decade Perspective." *Journal of Business Ethics* 91:457–465. doi 10.1007/s10551-009-0098-9.

Posner, Barry Z., and Warren H. Schmidt. 1992. "Values and the American Manager: An Update Updated." *California Management Review* 34 (3):80–94. doi: 10.2307/41167425.

Poswolsky, Adam Smiley. 2015. "What Millennial Employees Really Want." *Fast Company,* June 4. http://www.fastcompany.com/3046989/what-millennial-employees-really-want.

Prudential. n.d. "Prudential Careers." Prudential. Accessed November 21, 2016. http://jobs.prudential.com/?utm_medium=friendly&utm_source=redirect&utm_campaign=prudotcomjobs.

Pryce-Jones, Jessica. 2010. *Happiness at Work: Maximizing Your Psychological Capital for Success.* Hoboken, NJ: Wiley.

Pychyl, Timothy A. 2009. "Fear of Failure." *Psychology Today,* February. https://www.psychologytoday.com/blog/dont-delay/200902/fear-failure.

Rath, Tom. 2006. *Vital Friends: The People You Can't Afford to Live Without.* New York: Gallup Press.

Rehel, Erin, and Emily Baxter. 2015. "Men, Fathers, and Work-Family Balance." Center for American Progress, February 4. https://www.americanprogress.org/issues/women/reports/2015/02/04/105983/men-fathers-and-work-family-balance/.

Reid, Erin, and Lakshmi Ramarajan. 2016. "Managing the High Intensity Workplace." *Harvard Business Review,* June.

Rigoni, Brandon and Bailey Nelson. 2016. "Do Employees Really Know What's Expected of Them?" *Gallup Business Journal,* September 22. http://www.gallup.com/businessjournal/195803/employees-really-know-expected.aspx?g_source=EMPLOYEE_ENGAGEMENT&g_medium=topic&g_campaign=tiles.

Robison, Jennifer. 2010. "Disengagement Can Be Really Depressing." *Gallup Business Journal,* April 2. http://www.gallup.com/businessjournal/127100/disengagement-really-depressing.aspx.

Rones, Philip L., Randy E. Ilg, and Jennifer M. Gardner. 1997. "Trends in Hours of Work Since the Mid-1970s." *Monthly Labor Review,* April.

Rosen, Rebecca J. 2011. "Project Classroom: Transforming Our Schools for the Future." *The Atlantic,* August 29. http://www.theatlantic.com/technology/archive/2011/08/project-classroom-transforming-our-schools-for-the-future/244182/.

Rothman, Sheri, and Lee WanVeer. 2008. *Executive Coaching Fee Survey.* New York: The Conference Board.

Saad, Lydia. 2014. "The '40-Hour' Workweek is Actually Longer – by Seven Hours." Gallup Poll, August 29. http://www.gallup.com/poll/175286/hour-workweek-actually-longer-seven-hours.aspx.

Sahadi, Jeanne. 2015. "What Workers Around the World Want: More Flexibility." CNN Money, May 5. http://money.cnn.com/2015/05/05/pf/workplace-flexibility/.

Schulte, Brigid. 2014. *Overwhelmed: How to Work, Love, and Play When No One Has the Time*: New York: Sarah Chrichton Books.

Schwartz, Barry. 2015. *Why We Work.* New York: Simon & Schuster/TED Books.

Schwartz, Tony, and Christine Porath. 2014a. "Why You Hate Work." *New York Times,* May 30. http://www.nytimes.com/2014/06/01/opinion/sunday/why-you-hate-work.html.

————. 2014b. *The Human Era @ Work: Findings from the Energy Project and Harvard Business Review.* Yonkers, NY: The Energy Project.

Schwartz, Tony. 2011. "The Twelve Attributes of a Truly Great Place to Work." *Harvard Business Review,* September. https://hbr.org/2011/09/the-twelve-attributes-of-a-tru.html.

Setton, Mark K. n.d. "Ed Diener." The Pursuit of Happiness, Inc. http://www.pursuit-of-happiness.org/history-of-happiness/ed-diener/.

Sharpe, Steve. 2016. *Intuit 2020 Report: Twenty Trends that Will Shape the Next Decade.* Mountain View, CA: Intuit.

Shein, Edgar H. 1990. "Organzational Culture." *American Psychologist* 45 (2):109–119.

Shlain, Tiffany. 2012. "National Day of Unplugging: A Digital Detox." *The Huffington Post,* March 23.

Shoemaker, Jolynn, Amy Brown, and Rachel Barbour. 2011. "A Revolutionary Change: Making the Workplace More Flexible." *The Solutions Journal* 2 (2).

Sinek, Simon. 2009. *Start with Why: How Great Leaders Inspire Everyone to Take Action.* New York: Penguin Group.

Slaughter, Anne-Marie. 2012. "Why Women Still Can't Have It All." *The Atlantic,* July/August.

————. 2015. *Unfinished Business: Women Men Work Family.* New York: Random House.

Smith, Emily Esfahani. 2013. "There's More to Life Than Being Happy." *The Atlantic*, January 9. http://www.theatlantic.com/health/archive/2013/01/theres-more-to-life-than-being-happy/266805/.

Son, Sabrina. 2015. "Employee Engagement Surveys: The 20 Questions You Need to Ask." TINYpulse, October 7. https://www.tinypulse.com/blog/sk-employee-engagement-survey-questions.

Spurgeon, Anne, J. Malcolm Harrington, and Cary L. Cooper. 1997. "Health and Safety Problems Associated with Long Working Hours: A Review of the Current Position." *Occupational and Environmental Medicine* 54 (6):367–375.

Stefano, Giada Di, Francesca Gino, Gary P. Pisano, and Bradley R. Staats. 2016. *Making Experience Count: The Role of Reflection in Individual Learning*. Boston: Harvard Business School.

Stickgold, Robert, LaTanya James, and J. Allan Hobson. 2000. "Visual Discrimination Learning Requires Sleep After Training." *Nature Neuroscience* 3: 1237–1238. doi:10.1038/81756.

Stone, Douglas, Bruce Patton, and Sheila Heen. 1999. *Difficult Conversations: How to Discuss What Matters Most*. New York: Viking Adult.

Talbot, Danielle L., and Jon Billsberry. 2010. "Comparing and Contrasting Person-Environment Fit and Misfit." In *Exploring Organizational Fit and Misfit: Proceedings of the 4th Global e-Conference on Fit*. Milton Keynes, England: Open University.

Thorn, Andrew, Marilyn McLeod, and Marshall Goldsmith. 2007. *Peer Coaching Overview*. http://www.marshallgoldsmithfeedforward.com/docs/Peer-Coaching-Overview.pdf

Towers Watson. 2012. *Global Workforce Study*. Arlington, VA: Towers Watson. https://www.towerswatson.com/Insights/IC-Types/Survey-Research-Results/2012/07/2012-Towers-Watson-Global-Workforce-Study.

Twaronite, Karyn. 2015. *Global Generations: A Global Study on Work-Life Challenges Across Generations*. London: Ernest and Young Global Limited.

U.S. Department of Labor. 2014. "Charts from the American Time Use Survey." Bureau of Labor Statistics. http://www.bls.gov/tus/charts/home.htm.

———. 2015. "Number of Jobs Held, Labor Market Activity, and Earnings Growth Among the Youngest Baby Boomers: Results From a Longitudinal Survey," March 21. Bureau of Labor Statistics. http://www.bls.gov/news.release/pdf/nlsoy.pdf.

———. 2016. "Employment Situation Summary – October 2016." U.S. Department of Labor Bureau of Labor Statistics. http://www.bls.gov/news.release/empsit.nr0.htm

Vance, Robert J. 2006. *Employee Engagement and Commitment: A Guide to Understanding, Measuring and Increasing Engagement in Your Organization.* Alexandria, VA: Society for Human Resource Management.

Virgin Pulse 2015. *Misunderstood Millennials: How the Newest Workforce is Evolving Business.* Virgin Pulse, Inc.

Wade, Sophie. 2013. "The Changing Nature of Work (and What That Means for You)." *The Huffington Post,* September 13. http://www.huffingtonpost.com/sophie-wade/the-changing-nature-of-work-and-what-that-means-for-you_b_3915661.html.

Winkle-Giulioni, Julie. 2013. "Meaning Matters." Lead Change Group, March 4. http://leadchangegroup.com/meaning-matters/.

Wiseman, Theresa. 2015. "Four Attributes of Empathy." Too Good: Mendez Foundation, October 1. http://www.toogoodprograms.org/blog/four-attributes-of-empathy/.

Witters, Dan, and Sangeeta Agrawal. 2015. "Well-Being Enhances Benefits of Employee Engagement." *Gallup Business Journal,* October 27. http://www.gallup.com/businessjournal/186386/enhances-benefits-employee-engagement.aspx.

Work, Family, and Health Network. 2015. *Work, Family, and Health Study (WFHS).* Ann Arbor, MI: Inter-University Consortium for Political and Social Research (ICPSR) [distributor]. http://doi.org/10.3886/ICPSR36158. v1.

Wrzesniewski, Amy, Clark McCauley, Paul Rozin, and Barry Schwartz. 1997. "Jobs, Careers, and Callings: People's Relations to Their Work." *Journal of Research in Personality* 21:21–33.

Zappos. n.d. "Zappos Culture Book." Zappos Insights. Accessed November 21, 2016. https://www.zapposinsights.com/culture-book.

INDEX

ABOUT THE AUTHORS

Moe Carrick is Principal and Founder of Moementum, Inc., a Certified BCorp and consulting firm dedicated to the vision of creating a world that works for everyone, using business as a force for good. Her diverse client portfolio includes Prudential Financial, REI, ABB, Nike, Nintendo, Hydroflask, The Nature Conservancy, and others. Moe writes regularly for the Work Smart Blog and Conscious Company Media, and was a featured consultant in *Fast Company* magazine. A frequent presenter, she has spoken at South by Southwest (SXSW), TEDxPeachtree, TEDxSanJuan Island, the Women's Center for Leadership, the American Public Works Association, and the Human Resource Management Association. She is a Coach, a Certified Daring Way Facilitator, a Certified Senior Human Resource Professional, and holds an MS in Organizational Management from Antioch University.

Cammie Dunaway is a Global Chief Marketing Officer, Brand Consultant, and Public Board member. She most recently served as U.S. President and Global Chief Marketing Officer of KidZania. Previously she served as Executive Vice President of Sales and Marketing at Nintendo and as Chief Marketing Officer at Yahoo! after having spent more than a decade in various leadership positions with Frito Lay, where she was named one of the 100 Top Marketers by *Advertising Age*. Cammie sits on the Board of Directors for Nordstrom Bank, Red Robin, and Marketo. A frequent presenter, she has spoken at The Conference Board's Summit on Corporate Brand and Reputation, TEDxHarkerSchool, South by Southwest (SXSW), and Venture Beats Growth Conference, and for numerous companies including General Mills, LinkedIn, PayPal, and Unilever. She holds a BA from the University of Richmond and an MBA from Harvard Business School.